Stepping Up

The Recreational Player's Guide to Beating Casino and Internet Poker

S0-BZE-646

Randy Burgess

Other ConJelCo titles:

Books

Internet Poker: How to Play and Beat Online Poker Games
by Lou Krieger and Kathleen Keller Watterson

Hold'em Excellence: From *Beginner to Winner*
by Lou Krieger

Las Vegas Blackjack Diary
by Stuart Perry

More Hold'em Excellence: a Winner for Life
by Lou Krieger

Serious Poker
by Dan Kimberg

Video Poker—Optimum Play
by Dan Paymar

Winning Low-Limit Hold'em
by Lee Jones

Winning Omaha/8 Poker
by Mark Tenner and Lou Krieger

Software

Blackjack Trainer for the Macintosh or Windows

Ken Elliott's CrapSim for DOS

StatKing for Windows

Stepping Up

The Recreational Player's Guide to Beating Casino and Internet Poker

Randy Burgess

ConJelCo
Pittsburgh, Pennsylvania

Stepping Up: The Recreational Player's Guide to Beating Casino and Internet Poker
Copyright © 2003 by Randy Burgess

All rights reserved. This book may not be duplicated in any way or stored in an information retrieval system, without the express written consent of the publisher, except in the form of brief excerpts or quotations for the purpose of review. Making copies of this book, or any portion, for any purpose other than your own, is a violation of United States copyright laws.

Publisher's Cataloging-in-Publication Data

Burgess, Randy

Stepping Up: The Recreational Player's Guide to Beating Casino and Internet Poker
iv, 166p. ; 22cm.
ISBN 1-886070-18-0
I. Title.

Library of Congress Control Number: 2003114915

First Edition

1 3 5 7 9 8 6 4 2

Cover design by Melissa Hayden

ConJelCo LLC
1460 Bennington Ave
Pittsburgh, PA 15217
[412] 621-6040
http://www.conjelco.com

Table of Contents

Acknowledgements   ii
Foreword   iii

Section I: The Basics   **1**
1. The Missing Chapters   3
2. Key Differences between Casino Poker and
    Home Poker   13
3. Getting Started   22
4. Antes, Odds, and Outs: Theory You Can Use   35
5. Who to Study for Basic Strategy—and Who Not To   58

Section II: Playing the Other Players   **65**
6. Your Most Important Poker Weapon   67
7. Labeling Your Opponents   79
8. Reading Hands and Players in Hold'em   85
9. Reading Hands and Players in Stud   99
10. Reading Players with Tells   109

Section III: Getting Better   **115**
11. Avoiding Strategic Mistakes   117
12. Avoiding Physical and Emotional Mistakes   126
13. Refining Your Game   136
14. Glossary   152
15. Index   161
16. About the Author   164
17. About the Publisher   165

i

Acknowledgements

Carl Baldassarre, my primary poker buddy, needs to be thanked for many reasons: He encouraged me to write this book, accompanied me on many poker road trips, and more specifically, both reviewed and contributed to the chapter on reading hands in seven-card stud, his best game and my weakest. Learning poker wouldn't have been half as fun without Carl's support.

I'd also like to thank Scott "scottro" Harker, my editor at ConJelCo, for suggestions that made this book better throughout.

Finally, Katherine Burger, my life partner, also deserves thanks—in this context, chiefly for putting up with so much poker!

Foreword

I f you haven't bought this book yet I suggest you go to the cashier and make it yours. I have learned from it and I believe you will also.

This is not a step-by-step strategy, but a "thinking about poker" book that you'll hope your opponents won't read. My best-selling 7-Card Stud book, referred to in the text, is mostly strategy, with additional playing information I call the "stuff" of winning poker. Strategy and stuff—a winning combination. Randy's book is stuffed with "stuff."

What to learn more about reading hands and players? There are strong sections with a lot of good information for both 7 card stud and hold'em. Want to learn to avoid mistakes—both strategic and emotional? Randy points out that mistakes by your opponents are the number one reason you win at the low limits as a recreational player. It then follows that *your* mistakes are the main reason *you* lose at poker, whatever the limit. Randy includes a section of mistakes to avoid and to watch for in your opponents and adds, "Technical mistakes are still the ultimate cause of all losses—physical and emotional mistakes simply lead you to commit more technical errors than usual." He then comes at you with some very interesting information about "tells" you probably haven't thought of.

Randy stresses study and practice, as do I in my private poker lessons in Las Vegas. I quote one of my boyhood idols, All-American basketball player and NBA star, "Easy Ed" McCauley. *"When you are not practicing, someone, somewhere, is practicing. And when you meet, he will beat you."* Study Randy's work and you'll have a surprise for that fellow.

Even if you are an experienced player there is information here that you haven't thought of—and some that you used to know but have forgotten. Be reminded.

I don't know Randy Burgess—to my knowledge I've never laid eyes on him, and wouldn't know him if I tripped over him. But one day I will—not trip over him, but get to know him.

Another thing that I like about this book is that the title says very clearly and specifically what the book is about and what it will do for you. The home game and the public casino game are two different animals. This information will help you to make the transition smoothly.

I was very happy to see that Randy included a section titled "Your Most Important Poker Weapon," which is about observing your opponents to get a line on their play. Study it. Study it again. Learn it. The lad isn't kidding. It is that important. I stress the same objective to my students—"There is no substitute for knowledge of your opponents." He says it one way, I say it another, but we're both saying the same thing. We can't both be wrong. STUDY!!

Put bluntly, I wish I had written this book. So, if you'll excuse me, I'm going to read it again.

Roy West
Las Vegas poker teacher and Card Player columnist
September, 2003

Section 1

The Basics

Chapter 1

The Missing Chapters

W ho is this book for? If you consider yourself a recreational poker player interested in acquiring the skills to win, not just in your home game, but in cardrooms or on the Internet as well, then this book is for you. You're not an aspiring pro, but you want to play well enough to enjoy yourself in these more challenging environments.

This book is also for you if you're already a regular at public poker but frustrated with your results. You win now and then, but your losses add up to more than your winnings. At this point you'd be delighted just to break even.

And this book is *definitely* for you if you've tried to learn from poker books before now and been disappointed. There are basically three classes of poker books—advanced, beginner, and garbage. We'll ignore the garbage books for now. The advanced books can be fascinating, but typically they assume you already have a lot of poker experience and play at the medium limits or higher. Beginner books can seem helpful on first reading, but ultimately leave you feeling that the authors either didn't know enough or didn't tell you enough. If you're not only losing but don't know *why* you're losing, it's likely these beginner books didn't do their job.

It's almost as if there are chapters missing from all of these books. These chapters hold the information someone like you needs to succeed—so why has no one written them?

To answer that, let me tell you about my own adventures (or misadventures) as a poker novice. It might help you see what I came to see, and to understand why I wrote this book.

The lure of the big time

Throughout my twenties and thirties, I played more than my share of home poker—the usual nickel-ante affairs where as many cards are wild as possible and it's a matter of honor not to fold until the last possible moment. But the first time I ever set foot in a public cardroom was in 1998. I was driving up the highway through eastern Connecticut, on my way to Cape Cod for a vacation, when I saw the exit sign for the Foxwoods Casino. Maybe it was that I'd just read Herbert Yardley's "Education of a Poker Player," and my mind was still filled with the romance of old-time saloons and Hong Kong bordellos; whatever the reason, I had to stop and check it out.

Inside, Foxwoods looked more like a shopping mall or airport terminal than a glamorous casino. But once I'd squeezed past the hordes of tourists and found the poker room, I felt an immediate difference. The atmosphere was calming yet also exciting, like a good cup of coffee. Seeing the dozens of turquoise felt tables and the crowd of players seated at them heightened my excitement even more.

The only games within my budget that I recognized were Omaha high-low and seven-card stud. I settled on seven-card stud, and was beguiled by seeing my initials put down on a magic-marker whiteboard for the next available seat. I limited myself to $60 in chips, my goal being to see how long I could make them last.

The game was $1-$5 spread limit with a fifty-cent ante—big money by my home-game standards. But this was no home game. The dealer and my fellow players were quick to initiate me into the rules and rituals that seemed to matter so much to them: You could bet any amount between $1 and $5, but a raise had to be at least the amount of the previous bet. Calling and then raising was a "string raise," and you got your wrist slapped for it. If you won a pot, you tipped or "toked" the dealer; if you folded, you "mucked" your cards by tossing them toward the dealer rather than simply turning them over. And if you won a pot, the dealer asked to see *all* of your cards, not just the five that made up your hand.

The table, a sort of squashed oval, seemed too small at first; but soon I grew to like the close quarters and the feeling they inspired of immersion in another world, a magic green circle. My companions at the table were blue-collar retirees and housewives, yet there was a spirit of commonality I hadn't expected to find playing with strangers.

It took me two hours to lose my $60, but I was proud I'd lasted even that long. I won a few small pots but mostly my chips just seemed to dribble away. The only time I was dealt a good hand, three deuces "rolled up" (I wouldn't learn that term till much later), my excitement was so obvious that the entire table mucked in unison when I bet the maximum. I vowed to keep my cool next time, and make some money with those deuces.

Of course, before there *was* a next time, I needed to get better so I wouldn't be throwing my money away. No problem: There were plenty of books about poker—all I had to do was read them. Or so I thought.

Learning everything except winning

Over the course of the next two years, I bought, borrowed, and studied over two dozen poker books. They ranged from the friendly and entertaining "Thursday Night Poker" by Peter O. Steiner, who promised to teach me how to win in my weekly game but wasn't so sure about the casinos, to the intimidating "Seven-Card Stud for Advanced Players," which talked about "expert plays" in high-stakes games I would never play in. I cracked the silver covers of Doyle Brunson's classic "Super/System," but his advice seemed meant for future world champions in no-limit hold'em, not average guys like me. I studied the photographs in a book on tells by "Crazy Mike" Caro and tried to apply this knowledge to my home game: when Bob flicked his cards nervously, did that mean he'd made a big hand? When Thom covered his mouth with his hand, was he bluffing?

I learned how to calculate probabilities, hoping that the ability to compute the number of ways to make a full house would somehow carry over into a better sense of how to win at Baseball and Iron Cross. Taking a cue from David Sklansky's "Theory of Poker," I tried "semi-bluffing", but my only successful bluffs were when I misread my hand and semi-fooled everybody, including myself.

My results were what you would expect. Over the next two years in the home game I bobbed up and down, but mostly down, like a yo-yo on a badly wound string. On a return visit to Foxwoods I won $37 and decided I was catching on—until the next time, when I lost twice that much despite good cards.

I'd read more poker books than anyone else I knew, and I was a reasonably smart guy—so why wasn't I getting any better? The authors of the books I'd read were all experts, so *they* couldn't be wrong. It was my fault. Whatever intangible ingredient it took to win at poker, I didn't have it, and they couldn't teach it to me.

Getting lucky

Right before I decided to give up and stop studying poker forever, someone lent me one last book, a slim blue volume with the title of "Seven Card Stud: The Complete Course in Winning at Medium and Lower Limits." I hadn't come across it before, nor had I ever heard of the author, a guy wearing a cowboy hat on the back cover named Roy West. It took no time at all to read once through, and for me, it was a revelation. I'll unashamedly add that if you're a beginning stud player you ought to buy this book right now before reading another word of mine.

West teaches that the single most important key to winning, once you've learned a solid basic strategy, is playing the other players, not just your own cards. This means, among other things, studying how your opponents prefer to play various types of hands. For example, will they always raise with a big pair in seven-stud, or do they like to limp in? Will they raise on a flush draw, and if so, under what circumstances? If you're good at learning the tendencies of your opponents, you can often make an extremely educated guess at what hand your opponent is holding by the way he's betting it, almost as if he flipped his cards over to show you. And since the value of your own hand rises or falls based on your opponents' hands, such knowledge is worth more than almost anything else that's going on in the game.

Studying your opponents is essential to winning poker, and every good intermediate and advanced player knows it—yet West's is the *only* beginner's book I've ever come across that discusses it adequately. My guess is that good poker writers think it's too tough a concept for beginning players to handle, while bad poker writers don't know enough about it to speak with authority. As a result, studying opponents usually isn't talked about until you get to the advanced books, but there, it's presented in the context of expert plays not useful for a beginner.

Reading West started me on a two-year campaign of learning how to really play. His ideas gave me the tools and insights I needed to begin to decipher the advanced books and apply their ideas to the game situations I commonly encountered. Once I'd taught myself to reliably win at low-limit stud, I decided to learn hold'em, a game which had always baffled me before. Not surprisingly, the beginner books for hold'em left out a number of things I considered important, such as studying opponents. But by now I knew enough to start asking the right questions on my own.

What I won't teach you—and what I will

So why should you bother buying or reading this book, if West's book is such a hot ticket for the beginning player? To put it another way, what's this book about? How am I going to help your poker career?

I'll tell you right away that I'm *not* going to teach you basic street-by-street strategy for seven-stud, hold'em, or any other game. Why not? For one thing, there are a number of excellent introductory books for most of the commonly played games already in print, West's among them; I'm not going to waste your time or money covering the same ground. Besides, some of you may feel you already know the fundamentals and are no longer at the absolute beginner level. If so, great; you're ready to jump in without further ado. I'd advise at least skimming the rest of Section 1 to make sure you understand the terms and concepts I'll be using throughout the book. After that, you can tackle the more advanced material in Sections 2 and 3.

But what if you don't yet know the fundamentals for the game you want to play? In that case, plan on using Section 1 of this book as a study guide to accelerate your poker learning. I'll review the best of the books for beginners on individual games, including an analysis of any gaps in the material to watch out for. Plus, I'll give you tips for studying and practicing that you won't find anywhere else, along with immediately usable explanations of concepts like pot odds and expected value.

That's just the first step. Once you know the basics, you'll be ready to understand what I really have to teach you, starting in Section 2: how to become a *situationally based* player.

That's it, you ask? A situationally based player?

Pretend for a moment that you're a professional poker player, and think about it the way they do. You don't play poker against a deck of cards—you play it in the context of a situation. At its most complex, the situation includes more factors than your brain can consciously process, given how quickly you have to respond at the table. Typically, though, a handful of factors count the most: a sound basic strategy for the game in question; the relative sizes of the house rake, bets, antes, and blinds, often called the *structure*; your opponents' style of play, both as individuals and as a group; and a rough calculation of whether each decision you make has what's known as *positive expectation*—that is, whether it will win or lose you money. Not necessarily today, not necessarily tomorrow, but in the long run. A situationally based player looks at all of these factors and adjusts his play accordingly. He can play one way today and another way tomorrow, even though the game appears the same to an outsider.

The opposite of a situationally based player is what Mason Malmuth, one of the more abstract writers on today's poker scene, has called a "self-weighting" player. It's a fancy term for describing someone who plays the same way all the time, regardless of the situation. For "self-weighting," you could just as easily substitute "self-defeating." Yet this is the way most beginner books teach you to play!

Keep in mind that in your visits to the casinos, most players you see are losing players. This is true even of players who seem strong and fearless and are racking up a lot of chips on the day you happen to see them. It's as true of players at the middle and high limits as of players at the $1-$3 stud tables. It's true of players who talk a good game, too. I've sat at some tables and been impressed by some guy's poker talk—only to see him broadcast tells, go on tilt, misread hands, play too tight when he should have been playing loose, play too loose when he should have tightened up, and otherwise throw his money away.

So how do you become a winning, non-self-weighting, situationally based player? There are three ways. First, if you're naturally gifted, you don't have to read any books at all—you'll pick it up on your own. Very few people are this talented. Second, if you're like most amateur players I know, you can sweat it out over many months or even years before some isolated incident, person, or book finally gives you a clue as to what it's all about. If you're lucky, your own understanding may have matured enough by then so that you're able to recognize the clue for what it is. Otherwise that moment of discovery will go right over your head and it's back to the salt mines.

Then there's the third way—by reading this book.

In a nutshell, it's my intent to show you concepts and techniques often discussed in advanced books, but rarely presented in beginning poker books. These are the missing chapters. This is the information you need in order to enjoy success over the long term, regardless of whether you win or lose in a particular session. In fact, once you learn these concepts, how much you win or lose on any given day will become much less important to you.

It's my contention that an intelligent recreational player—someone who's played a lot of poker in a home game, for example—is more than ready for these concepts and techniques, as long as they're presented at an appropriate level. While much of what the top writers have to say is genuinely too complex for all but a handful of professionals and high-level amateurs, we'll talk here only about the stuff you *can* learn and use.

I've culled this material from the best of poker literature today, as well as from my own experience as a successful recreational player in learning what works and what doesn't. The key is that while expert writers present this material in the context of big-money games and sophisticated plays, I've gone in the opposite direction: I've created clear but correct explanations and examples to fit the lower-limit games you'll find yourself playing in at the beginning of your public poker career. As a bonus, I'll talk about how these concepts can help you win in your home game as well.

To further whet your appetite, here are a few more things we'll be covering, in addition to the advanced concepts already mentioned:

- The difference between home poker and casino poker. We'll discuss the rake, the blinds or ante, the nature of your opponents, and other factors that make casino poker more difficult to beat.

- Tips for learning as inexpensively as possible by practicing with commercial software such as Turbo Stud and Turbo Hold'em from Wilson Software, or by playing in the inexpensive "micro-limit" live games available online.

- Common types of opponents you'll encounter in a public cardroom, and how to play against them. This includes interpreting their behavior so that you can often duck their strong hands, whereas a self-weighting player will walk right into them.

- The truth about tells. It's not what you read in most poker books.

- How to track and correct your mistakes as you learn. You win at low-limit poker mostly by avoiding mistakes at the table while encouraging other players to make them. In addition, there are mental and emotional mistakes to beware of, such as playing when you're tired, jet-lagged, or upset. I'll share the techniques I've developed for guarding against these traps.

- Probability, odds, and mathematical expectation as they apply to poker. If you're afraid of the math, don't be—I'm terrible at math myself and yet I've made big strides in this area by slowly learning what I can, when I can.

That's the program: the same methods I used to transform myself into a successful low-limit winner at Foxwoods and other casinos, online, and in the two home games I play.

What's the bottom line here? I think of it like this: I'll never earn enough as a recreational poker player to pay for a new boat or an addition to my house, but I'm doing well enough to splurge on a fancy dinner every now and then. I'm also slowly building my bankroll. I'm meeting the goals I set early on: to enjoy myself, to learn a new aspect of the game every so often, and to keep improving. If you're willing to put in some time away from the table studying and practicing, you can do the same. My only warning is that it takes not only time but some hard work—but you expected that, didn't you?

Let's get started.

Chapter 2

Key Differences between Casino Poker and Home Poker

If your home game is like mine, everybody plays pretty loose. It's a social occasion with lots of chat and plenty of interruptions, and no one is really out for blood, even if the losers do pout some. It's a very relaxed event.

Even if you've never been to a casino, you can guess it's much different. Understanding exactly how and why it's different can save you from some of the more painful beginner faux paux, while also providing useful insights into opponents. For those of you who *have* been to public cardrooms and feel you know the ropes, consider skimming this chapter anyway as a review.

To start with, home poker is informal, but poker in a public cardroom is formal—as formal in its own way as trial by jury or a nineteenth century English dance. Minor infractions of the rules in a home game, such as betting out of turn or declaring high when you meant to go low, are punished by no more than good-natured jeering. But in a casino, similar violations can result in penalties ranging from the relatively minor disaster of forfeiting a pot you would have otherwise won, all the way to being permanently banned from a cardroom. Fortunately, observing the rules is easy once you know them. More on that later.

It goes without saying that you won't be drinking any alcohol at the table. If your goal is to win, you don't want to impair your judgment in the slightest. Even so, you'll most likely find you're not immune to the tide of animosity. Losing in a casino hurts much more than losing in a home game, since the stakes are higher and winning is likely to be a prime goal for you.

Behaving well when you're losing is important, not only out of courtesy to others, but in order to keep the emotional sanity that you need for the long term. Another difference is that where home poker is played with a smile, casino poker is frequently played with a scowl. Players sometimes take out what they perceive to be their bad luck by cursing opponents, throwing cards at the dealer, and so on. (Be warned that repeatedly mistreating a dealer is a good way to get yourself barred from the poker room.) A number of these sore losers will also be drunk, since cardrooms typically offer free drinks to players.

How about the social aspect of the game? Here too, things are different. It's true that if you frequent the same cardroom, you'll discover that some players are regulars who know each other well and treat the game like a party. But you'll also discover that the best players are usually not the noisy ones gabbing with their buddies, but the quiet ones watching the rest of the table. It's good to be friendly with your fellow players, but friendly isn't the same thing as social. If you want to win, fulfill your needs for friendship and partying somewhere else, not in a cardroom.

Other important differences, such as the need to play tight compared to a home game, are covered in Chapter 4, "Antes, Odds, and Outs: Theory You Can Use" on page 35. Likewise, the complete cast of characters you're likely to encounter at the public poker table is covered in Chapter 7, "Labeling Your Opponents" on page 79. For now, let's look at the rules of play for a typical public cardroom, why these rules exist, and how to abide by them.

Poker rules, poker rituals

A lot of poker room rules are game-specific, such as the requirement in seven-stud that the low card showing after the deal must "bring it in" by betting a specified minimum amount or more. You'll pick up such rules quickly enough on your own as you read and practice. Here, we're going to focus only on the most important rules and points of etiquette—those that define public poker.

Eventually, these rules and rituals will come to feel not only natural but necessary. Sloppily run cardrooms have slow games with lots of arguments and dealer abuse; a top cardroom like the Bellagio or The Mirage in Las Vegas makes it a pleasure to play by enforcing the rules and keeping the action fast and smooth.

Sign up for the game you want when you arrive at the cardroom.

You'll learn this part on your first casino trip, but here are some additional tips to smooth the way.

Low-limit games generally don't accept reservations, so you have to wait till you get to the cardroom to actually sign up for a game. If you're visiting a club or very small casino where the action is slow (say, during the morning on a weekday), it's worth calling in advance to ask when the games get busy. When you get to the casino, you'll sign up by asking the poker room desk or a floor supervisor to put your initials down for the game you want. The desk will tell you if there's open seating available, meaning you can play right away; if not, they can give you a good idea of how soon a seat is likely to open up. In a crowded poker room, I like to give all three of my initials (RAB) so I don't get confused with any other RBs out there. If you get comfortable with more than one limit or form of casino poker, you'll often play in an open game while waiting for a seat in your preferred game. Just keep an ear out for the PA announcements to make sure you hear your initials called.

In some cardrooms you can ask the desk to "lock up" a seat in a game when it comes open. This reserves it for you if you happen to be temporarily out of the cardroom when your initials are called. At a recent morning visit to the Bellagio, for example, I put down a small deposit to lock up a seat so I could get breakfast rather than hang out twiddling my thumbs. At other cardrooms, however, players seem to ask the floor to "lock up" a seat only when they want to play out a hand in their current game before moving to the seat that just came open in their preferred game. Ask the management of your particular cardroom what the options are.

Act in turn, whether you're checking, folding, betting, or raising.

Acting out of turn is common in home games, but it's not tolerated in the casino. People will jump on you if you do it, starting with the dealer, who needs to keep strict control of the action and the money going into the pot. The player you've interrupted may feel you've interfered with his decision-making, and he might even suspect you of being an "angle-shooter"—someone who tries to gain advantage with tricks like faking an out-of-turn fold, then raising.

On the flip side, acting in turn makes it easier for you to concentrate on things that really matter to your game. For example, it's easier to keep track of the pot size as each player calls or raises in order. And since pot size is one of the most important things to think about, that's no small benefit.

No string bets.

In many home games, it's accepted practice to call before raising—saying, for example, "I'll see your fifty cents—and raise you fifty!" This is known as a string bet, and in public poker, it's verboten. Try it in a casino game and the dealer will immediately tell you to pull back any chips you raised with; you will be permitted only to call. If you want to raise, you must say so and put all your chips (the amount of the call plus the amount of the raise) forward at once. In many cases you don't even have to speak; you can just put forward the requisite chips and everyone will understand you mean raise. If there is any doubt—for example, you've run out of smaller chips to merely call with—the dealer will ask you if you're raising or calling.

Don't splash the pot.

When you're betting, calling, or raising, put your chips slightly towards the center of the table, but still in front of your hand. Do *not* throw them in the middle or directly into the pot, as you would in a home game. The dealer needs to be able to track each bet, take out the rake, make change, adjust for any side pots if players are all-in, and so on; splashing the pot, as it's called, just confuses the issue.

Muck your cards properly.

If you're folding, throw your cards face down towards the dealer so she can gather them in. All you need is a flick of the wrist. Actually throwing your cards *at* the dealer is considered rude, as is not throwing them far enough and making her reach for them or beg you to throw them in. Many players who have chosen to blame the dealer for their losses will continually try this trick of not throwing their cards in far enough; do it too often and a good dealer will call a floor supervisor and have you scolded.

Protect your hand.

Be aware that if your hole cards are touched by cards that have been mucked by another player, your hand will be considered dead: the dealer is not required to distinguish between your face-down cards and the mucked cards, which are also face down. Therefore, you must protect your hand. You do this by putting a chip or other object on top of your cards; this keeps them from getting knocked loose or confused with any mucked cards that come your way. Regulars often have a favorite trinket for this purpose, such as a heavy foreign coin or special chip. But a chip or two on top of your cards is good enough.

Learn to look at your hand without showing anyone else.

This isn't a rule, but it relates to protecting your hand. In a home game, players pick up their hole cards and may even hold them out of sight below the table. Not only is holding cards out of sight forbidden in a public cardroom, you should also get out of the habit of picking them off the table at all. It's too easy for someone to see part of your hand that way. If you haven't already, learn how to pry up the near corners with your thumb, while keeping the rest of the cards flat on the table and cupping your palms to shield the view. If you're unsure of how to accomplish this, simply watch the other players.

Show all *your cards at showdown.*

In a home game you declare your own hand, and typically show only the five cards that make it up. But in a cardroom, it's the dealer's job to declare the winning hand, and she will need to see every card you've got. This practice protects all players at the table, including you. Of course, if the dealer misdeclares the winner (dealers get tired too), you can step in and make this known. Don't be afraid to speak up; you have the right to question decisions at the table, and if you're not satisfied with those decisions, you have the right to request the decision of a floorman. Just remember to be polite to everyone involved, including the possibly erring dealer.

Remember that once you muck your hand it's gone, even if you accidentally muck a royal flush. If you've paid money for the showdown, you're better off putting your cards face up for the dealer to see. A lot of players automatically muck losing hands so opponents can't see what they were betting on—but they're often the same players who every now and then realize too late that they've mucked the winning hand because they "knew" they were beat. Don't let this be you. Once you've gained experience, you can begin to muck your clearly beaten hands—but if you have any doubt at all about a hand, show it down.

Be aware that at some cardrooms, any player involved in any stage of the hand can ask to see your cards if you paid to see the showdown. This rule is meant to discourage a form of collusion in which a player with a garbage hand will hang in there to the river, betting and raising to build the pot for his buddy, who has secretly signaled that he has a monster. This sort of cheating doesn't happen very often, but is potentially dangerous, especially in high-low games. For the sake of politeness, if a player who didn't see the showdown asks to see your losing hand before you muck it, go ahead and show it to him. If he asks again and gets obnoxious about it, you can ask the floor to intervene and tell him not to abuse this rule. It's meant solely to discourage cheating, not to give other players a free look at your cards whenever they want.

Tip the dealer, but not too much.

Tipping the dealer isn't required, but if you don't do it you'll hear some poorly-concealed bitching as he or she departs and the new dealer arrives: "Seat five is dead, Sid. Absolutely dead." Whether a dealer *deserves* to be tipped is another question; good dealers move the game along, but both good and bad dealers seem to get tipped equally as far as I can see.

But although you should tip, you are justified in keeping the cost down to the minimum, since it comes out of your bankroll. For example, if you're sitting in a $3-$6 hold'em game, you're not obliged to toss the dealer a $1 chip each time you win a pot; go to the cashier's window and buy a roll of half dollars and tip fifty cents instead. No dealer can object to this, and you'll save money. It's customary when you win a monster pot to tip the dealer somewhat more; likewise, if you win a very small pot, you're not expected to tip at all. As you move up in limit, adjust your tip size accordingly, but don't feel obliged to be a big tipper at any time.

Ask the dealer to resolve any disputes.

If you think something isn't cricket—anything from the way a hand was dealt to a dispute with a fellow player—notify the dealer and ask them to rule on the situation. If the dealer isn't sure how to proceed, they'll call the floor over for an official ruling.

Keep enough money on the table to play properly.

In public poker, you're only permitted to gamble with the money you have on the table when a hand starts. You can't take your chips off the table during a deal, and you can't pull a hundred-dollar bill out of your wallet and throw it onto the felt when you discover the last card gave you a monster hand. This rule leads to a situation called "going all-in," in which the player doesn't have enough money to call further bets. When this occurs, a side-pot is created. Bad low-limit players are constantly going all-in, even if they intend to buy more chips after they bust out. They like the excitement of relinquishing control combined with the safety of limited financial risk—but it's bad poker. If you can't bet or raise the maximum, you can't protect a hand that might win the pot if you could knock other players out. Worse, if you make a big hand, you win only the main pot with which you were initially involved, not the side pot—even if said side pot gets as big as a mountain on later betting rounds in which you can't participate.

This leads to three simple rules:

- Always make your buy-in big enough for the limit. Generally I like to have at least 20 to 30 big bets on hand when I sit down for a session. For example, $120 to $180 is my minimum buy-in for a $3/$6 limit game. Anything less doesn't give me enough maneuvering room to handle the inevitable ups and downs, and also leaves me open to aggressive players who may target me as short-stacked and try to run me over by constantly raising my bring-in or blind.

- If you're losing but genuinely feel the game is soft and you're playing well, make sure you buy more chips before you get that big hand, not after.

- If you're losing and perhaps playing less than your best game, don't be afraid to quit before you lose all your chips. There's absolutely no need to go all-in and walk away broke. Your goal is to improve your poker and have fun, not punish yourself emotionally or financially.

Take breaks, but don't exceed the time limit.

Once you're seated at your game you'll want to take breaks fairly frequently, whether to clear your head, talk strategy with a buddy, or get dinner. It's fine to leave your chips and money on the table, but be wary about leaving anything you value on your seat or on the little side trolleys that hold meals and drinks. Trolleys get moved around, the cleaning crew doesn't always do a good job of realizing what's garbage and what's not, and a player with loose fingers may decide that whatever you left on your seat looks interesting.

Most cardrooms place a limit on how long you can be away from the table; generally this amounts to two dealer shifts of 30 minutes each, for a total of an hour. After that, the floor is liable to come along and bag your chips to make room for anyone on the waiting list. You'll have to get your chips back from management, and you'll have lost your playing seat. Beyond that, it's rude to keep others from playing when know you're not going to be playing yourself. A game can even break up if too many players are absent from the table but haven't given up their seats.

Chapter 3

Getting Started

I n a home game, it's easy to pick up a new variety of poker: one of your buddies tells you the rules, and you start playing without further ado. Because the stakes are so low, it's hard to get hurt by jumping right in. But this approach won't work for casino poker, where the stakes are higher, the players are more serious about taking your money, and the house is getting its cut too. Far better to do some reading and practicing beforehand—you'll lose less and enjoy yourself more. With this in mind, I suggest the following plan of study:

1. Pick the game you want to learn.

2. Read this book straight through once—you can refer back to various chapters as necessary.

3. Learn the basic strategy for your game by reading one or two good beginner books on it.

4. Practice inexpensively before you play, either with software or in the very low-limit games available online.

5. Start playing for real at a casino or club, at a limit that's affordable for you.

6. Keep track of your results; analyze your mistakes and successes.

7. Refer back to this book as necessary. You'll find yourself rereading Section 3 in particular, with its emphasis on refining your game, eliminating mistakes, and taking the long view.

How long will all this take you? Obviously that depends on how much free time you can spare for what is essentially a hobby. If you're willing to put in a lot of overtime, a week or two might be enough; scratched out here and there, it might take you longer, say a month or two. In any case, the quickest way to gauge your progress and get a sense of whether you're ready to start gambling for real will come from the practicing you do in step four. Let's go over each of the steps in turn to see how we build up to that point.

1. Pick the game you want to learn.

You've probably already made this decision. If you haven't, here are some thoughts.

The games most commonly available at casinos and clubs are hold'em, seven-card stud, Omaha high-low, and seven-card-stud high-low. Call the casino or club you plan to play at to ask them which games they spread at low limits, and what those limits are. And ask them how often they spread these games— you might find, for example, that they although they *say* they offer Omaha and stud high-low, they do so only sporadically, whenever they can get enough players to make up a table.

Beyond simple availability, there are other factors to consider. If you've played both stud and hold'em in your home game, you know which you like, and you can make your decision on that basis. Many beginners find stud easier to play because it seems to make sense, whereas hold'em can seem counter-intuitive until you learn the concepts. Stud has another advantage in that many casinos spread their absolute lowest limits at stud—for example, $1-$3 or $1-$5 spread limit, versus $3-$6 structured limit for hold'em.[1] Unfortunately the rake at such miniscule limits is brutal; we'll talk more about the impact of

---

1. In a spread-limit game, you can bet any amount between the minimum and the maximum. For example, in a $1-$5 spread-limit stud game, you can bet as little as $1, as much as $5, or any amount in between. In a structured limit game, the bet sizes are predetermined. For example, in a $4-$8 hold'em game, you must bet or raise exactly $4 on the first two rounds, and exactly $8 on the following two rounds.

that in Chapter 4, "Antes, Odds, and Outs: Theory You Can Use," on page 35.[2]

High-low Omaha and stud are both fun games, and they may seem attractive if you've played a lot of high-low poker in your home game—but I'd recommend against them when you're just starting out. One of the big weaknesses of the novice casino player is playing too loose, and high-low forms of poker encourage this tendency. They're good games to learn once you know how to play tight and exploit looseness on the part of others—but until then, stay away. Nonetheless, if you're determined to go that route, I'll mention a couple of good books on these games in Chapter 5. That should keep the damage to a minimum.

Online poker offers further options in the form of both pot-limit and no-limit hold'em and stud, often with very small antes or blinds to keep the cost reasonable. These are fascinating forms of poker, but unless you regularly play in a pot-limit home game, I'd again advise holding off until you learn to play limit poker well. I'm not going to address pot-limit or no-limit in this book, since they're such different animals.

2. Read this book straight through first, then come back to it as a reference when needed.

Let's say you've decided to study hold'em: you've played it a lot in your home game, and although you still don't know the finer points, it has a lot of appeal for you. The first time through this book, the chapter on reading hands in hold'em is likely to be over your head. Skim it anyway, so you have an idea of what's there. Later, after you've digested the basic hold'em books I'll be recommending in the next chapter, you can revisit the material on reading hands and see how it can really improve your play.

---

2. *Rake* is the house cut. Incidentally, if I don't immediately explain a term, you can almost always find it in the glossary in the back of the book.

3. Learn basic strategy for your game by reading one or two good beginner books on it.
We'll go into this in detail in Chapter 5, "Getting Started," on page 22. I'll recommend the best books available—the ones you can't go far wrong with, as opposed to all the lousy books that sit on the bookstore shelves right next to the good ones, and that will in effect have you throwing your wallet on the table for the other players to riffle through at their leisure. Put simply, I'll save you money and time by recommending who to read and who to avoid.

4. Practice inexpensively before you play, either with software or at the lowest limits online.
In the old days—say, twenty years ago—you could only practice on your own or with a buddy by dealing out cards from a deck and pretending to play hands against each other. Now there are more efficient ways to learn without spending a lot of money, although dealing out hands can still be an informative exercise.

It's widely agreed that the best software for practicing poker is the Wilson Software "Turbo" lineup, including Turbo 7-Card Stud, Turbo Texas Hold'em, Turbo Omaha High-Low Split, and so on. Poker programs by other companies do exist but have received poor reviews.

The Wilson products are relatively inexpensive—for example, at the time I'm writing this, you can get Turbo Hold'em Version 5.0 for under $100—and they do a pretty good job with their simulated computer players. They allow you to change lineups—for example, you can go from a loose-aggressive table to a tight-passive table—as well as set different bet sizes, antes, and rakes, to duplicate play at different limits.

Poker software of this sort has its advantages and disadvantages. First, the advantages:

- You can play a lot of hands in a short time to gain experience more quickly than you would in real life. This is especially useful when you're learning a new game.

- As I mentioned above, you can experiment with adjusting your strategy for different lineups—aggressive versus passive, loose versus tight, and so on. For example, a few hundred hands of Turbo Stud against a loose lineup will quickly demonstrate to you the drastically increased need for live cards, as opposed to a tight game where a hand like a pair of Jacks with one dead Jack might still be playable on Third Street.

- For seven-card stud in particular, you can quickly get in a lot of practice remembering folded cards on all streets, allowing you to gauge the liveness of both your own cards and your opponents' cards. This is an essential skill in becoming a good stud player.

- You can develop your hand-reading skills by analyzing the computer players. You can start classifying them as tight versus loose, passive versus aggressive, etc., and also pick up on how they play specific types of hands. This is just what I'll teach you to do with real players in Section 2 of this book.

Now for the disadvantages:

- The computer players (at least in current versions of the programs) never learn, so you can cheat by doing things like always raising under the gun in hold'em. You have to restrain yourself from just playing to beat the machine.

- Because hands are dealt so quickly (with the option to zip through hands you don't want to play), the software encourages you to play rapidly and mechanically rather than think things through. This is one of the worst habits you can develop. I strongly encourage you *not* to zip through hands, at least not all the time. In fact, once you've got the hang of a game, I recommend making your play on the computer as realistic as possible by setting the time delay for computer players to something like one second rather than a tenth of a second. Use the software to slow down and practice your full range of skills, rather than treating it like a quick-action video game.

- The simulated games don't capture the intensity of live games, whether online or at a casino. You never feel you're engaged in a real test of will and skill—because in fact, you aren't. In fact, above a certain level of skill, the software may actually hurt your feel for real poker.

- To sum up, the Wilson products are an excellent learning tool for beginners and for more experienced players who want to use the software's custom programming capabilities to explore specific questions—say, whether a particular marginal starting hand is profitable and under what circumstances. However, they aren't a substitute for live play and must be used cautiously to avoid developing bad habits. Personally, I own both the stud and hold'em versions, and I plan to buy the Omaha version soon to brush up my skills for that game, since I've found a local club that spreads it frequently.

Online poker

By now there are entire books devoted to online poker—for example, "Internet Poker: How to Play and Beat Online Poker Games," by Lou Krieger and Kathleen Keller Watterson, published by ConJelCo. However, poker is poker, and if you learn to play a particular game well in the casino, you can apply the same skills and concepts online. The reverse is not entirely true: although playing well online will indeed help you in the casino, live play involves a few extra skills—most notably, reading tells and interacting socially with your opponents. There are other differences as well; for example, it's easier to go on tilt online because the action is so much quicker and there is no fear of public embarrassment to restrain you.

Online poker is an inexpensive way to learn a new game because most venues offer very low limits, such as $.50/$1 for hold'em, or no-ante $.25/$.50 seven-card stud. These games are usually very loose and weak, but that doesn't mean it's easy to beat them if you're just starting out. In fact, one of the most common types of posts on poker forums like Two Plus Two (www.twoplustwo.com) is some guy moaning that he can't beat the $1-$2 hold'em game at Paradise, and is thinking of moving up because he's heard tighter, bigger games are easier to beat. The truth is, of course, that if you can't beat a loose game with a low rake and moronic opposition, you're not ready to move up. Learn the proper strategy to beat that terrible game, and then inch up the limits, learning how to compensate at each level for increasingly tougher or trickier opposition. That's what I did when I set out to learn hold'em. Over the course of a year playing hold'em on Paradise Poker, I worked my way up from $.50/$1 ring games to $5-$10 short-handed and ring games, where I still am at the time of writing. (By the way, *ring* means a full table of seven to ten players, while *short-handed* means six or fewer players. Online poker is unique in regularly offering short-handed and head-up opportunities that you won't always find in a casino.)

Some cautions about online play: Because it's so easily and immediately accessible, it can become addictive, to the detriment of both your poker and your life. I ran into this problem early on in my online poker career, when I fell into the trap of playing nearly every day for many hours at a time. My concentration suffered, and I started experiencing big swings instead of the steady wins I'd been accustomed to. The answer was to cut back to a more realistic playing schedule, one that leaves plenty of time for having a life.

I believe online addiction is fairly common and can afflict even someone who is otherwise balanced and disciplined. During those periods when I'm playing online regularly, I see the same names at the tables day after day—and most of these players lose continually, sometimes heavily. The lesson? Use online poker to learn a new game or keep up your skills, but be alert for any signs of overdoing it. Don't get sucked into a losing spiral. And if you can't ration your playing time, quit playing online and stick to live poker. It's much harder to overdose on.

That said, here's a short introduction to online poker as learning tool.

Finding a game. Two of the top poker sites at the time of writing are Paradise Poker (www.paradisepoker.com) and Poker-Stars (www.pokerstars.com). However, there are lots of others, some of which reportedly offer special buy-in deals or ultra-ultra-low limits. Your best bet is to visit a reputable poker forum such as the rec.gambling.poker newsgroup or TwoPlusTwo (www.twoplustwo.com) and read the most recent posts as to where people are playing online and what they think of those sites.

Play money versus real money. Play money tables aren't realistic, but they're handy for getting a feel for a poker site's user interface at zero cost—what buttons to click, how to make notes on players, customize the screen or sound effects, etc. Once you've gotten comfortable with the settings, switch over to the micro-limits and start playing real poker, albeit for tiny stakes. I'm assuming you can afford to spend something like $50 on your initial stake for a $.50/$1 limit game—that's fifty big bets, which should be enough to keep you going for a while.

Buying in. At the time of writing, some members of Congress are trying to legislate against U.S. banks or institutions lending money to people who play at poker sites or other online gambling sites. The sites themselves are all offshore, so they can't be legislated against; the only weak link is the transfer of funds. Such bills have been proposed in the past and gone down to defeat, but someday one may get through. It's likely at that point that players and sites will find a workaround to keep things going. The morality of online poker shouldn't bother anyone when our state governments are so heavily involved in running gambling of their own in the form of lotteries.

At any rate, you can fund your stake in an online poker game by going through Internet credit sites such as Firepay (www.firepay.com) or NetTeller (www.neteller.com). Such sites ascertain the legitimacy of your bank account by placing a small deposit for a certain number of cents in the account. Once you verify having received this exact sum, you are authorized to transfer money from that bank account to your online account; you can then transfer from your online account to an account at your chosen poker site. There are other ways of funding, such as wire transfers or sending in a check, but I haven't found the need to resort to them.

Taking notes. Most online poker interfaces offer a "notes" feature in which right-clicking your mouse on an opponent's name, or some similar action, will open a small text box in which you can type your observations: "Prefers to limp big wired pairs, waits till the big bet on Fifth Street to raise." "Can be induced to bluff." "Slowplays strong hands, raises flop with top pair bad kicker or second pair." Taking notes is an excellent way to reinforce the habit of analyzing opponents. And as we'll discuss further in Section 2, developing this habit is crucial to success.

Other tools. If you play Paradise Poker, there's a database program called PokerStat that is available for very little money at www.thsoftware.com/pokerstat. Once you've set it up, it tracks your online playing statistics—for example, how much you've won or lost with each type of starting hand you've been dealt. Personally I find thinking and reading about the game to be more useful than PokerStat, but others rave about it, so you might want to check it out.

Concentrate on one game at a time. Most of your time playing online poker will be spent folding hands, just like in real life. This can become boring in a hurry, so you may get the bright idea of playing two tables at once. Don't do it—at least when you're just starting out. Researchers have demonstrated that multitasking results in poorer performance, even if you're not aware of it.[3] Beyond that, you can't study opposing players if you're not around to watch their play when you're out of the hand. For the same reasons, don't have the television on as you play, and don't try reading a book or paying bills in between hands. Even though you're sitting at a computer screen in your home rather than at a public poker table, you need to devote *all* your attention to the game.

What about collusion? Many people worry that online poker makes it too easy for a couple of players to sit down in the same game and do things like jam the pot when one player has a good hand and the other has garbage, trapping unsuspecting players in the middle. Chat software obviously allows colluders to exchange information about their hands, but I've never been very worried about this and have never seen any evidence of collusion. Reputable online poker sites such as Paradise use software to search for repeated patterns of play indicating possible collusion between one or more players. The above scenario, where two players cooperate in jamming the pot but one has a garbage hand, is one that over time would be detected by such a collusion algorithm.

5. Start playing for real.
There are two ways to determine if you're ready to start playing for meaningful stakes at your chosen game. First, the Wilson software products have a "challenge" feature, whereby

---

3. My source is "Multitasking Makes You Stupid: Studies Show Pitfalls of Doing Too Much at Once," by Sue Shellenbarger, Wall Street Journal, Feb. 27, 2003. You can probably still find this article if you do a Web search.

you play the same 50 or 100 hands as the program's best player so you can compare results. Once you consistently start winning this competition, you're probably ready to play for real. It doesn't mean you'll do as well against human competition, however—the computer is always easier to beat than live opponents. Second, if you're doing well at the micro-limits, you can safely move up to low limits like $1-$5, $3-$6, and so on, whether online or at a casino. This is the real thing; take a deep breath, reread Chapter 2 if you need to, and dive in.

6. Keep track of your results; analyze your mistakes and successes.

Unless you keep good records of every poker session you play, you can't know how you're doing and whether you're getting better. Here's how I do it.

I take a notebook with me when I play at a club or casino, and record the place, the date, my starting and finishing times, the limit, and how much I win or lose. From my starting and finishing times I calculate how many hours I played that session. This is better than just writing down your win or loss per session, since some sessions may be short and others long. If during a session I feel I've just misplayed a hand, I step away from the table to write it down, so I can review it later and think about how to play such hands better. Lastly, as I've already mentioned, I often step away from the table to write down notes on opponents and help my hand-reading.

Once I'm back home, I enter my hours and win or loss into a software program to keep track of them for the long term. I use a program called StatKing, published by ConJelCo; it's built for this purpose and is very convenient. You can sort your entries by different limits and places, for example to see how you're doing on online poker versus casino poker, or at $3/$6 hold'em versus $5/$10 hold'em. If you want to keep initial costs down you can use an Excel spreadsheet, or if you hate software, you can just keep your records on paper. But keep records you must.

Keeping records will help for another reason: it will better help you cope with that nasty poker demon named "variance." We'll talk more about variance in Chapter 4, "Antes, Odds, and Outs: Theory You Can Use." For now, just realize that even if you play a consistently winning style of poker, you can have many sessions in a row where you lose—or many sessions in a row where you win. In the short term, poker is like a rubber ball bouncing up and down, and bouncing you with it. It's only over the long term, meaning hundreds of hours, that you can tell whether you're beating the game and whether you're getting better.

To see beyond the mirage of variance, you must average out your long-term results to see how much you're winning or losing, not per session, but per hour. Your unit of measurement isn't dollars (since you will probably be playing at more than one limit over the course of a year) but big bets, since this is always proportional to the limit. The result is known in poker parlance as your hourly rate. If after a year of playing regularly your hourly rate is better than when you started, you're improving. If not, you may have hit a particularly prolonged streak of negative variance—or more likely, there is something wrong with your strategy and tactics which you must work on fixing.

Let's bring up another poker term here—your bankroll. Professional players have bankrolls which constitute their working capital; they need a healthy bankroll to compete at a given limit to avoid gambling with the rent money. You shouldn't gamble with your rent money either, but it's more likely when you're just starting out that you'll finance your poker as you would any hobby—throwing some spare cash in that direction as you need to and as you feel you can afford it. But as soon as you can, you should think about establishing a bankroll just as a professional would, albeit on a smaller scale. It will help your mental discipline and give you confidence once you see that you're building it steadily over time.

How big a bankroll should you maintain for a given limit? Poker authorities like David Sklansky, Mason Malmuth, and Bob Ciaffone have written at length about this subject. For playing at the low limits, where you hope to have a real edge on weak opposition, 200 big bets should be enough sufficient to keep you from going broke during stretches of bad beats, bad cards, or bad play; for example, an initial bankroll of $1,000 should be sufficient for $1-$5 spread-limit stud. If you were a professional playing for a living against tough opponents, this probably wouldn't be enough—but since you're not and can afford a little more risk, 200 big bets should be more than adequate. As you start to move up to approach the middle limits, you may want to extend that to 300 big bets—but there's time for that later.

Don't lose heart if you get hammered your first few sessions out of the gate, or even your first few months; just keep reviewing your play to see how you can improve. Don't be in a hurry to win back any losses; be in a hurry to be patient and keep learning. We'll talk more about catching and correcting mistakes in Chapter 11, "Avoiding Strategic Mistakes." And we'll talk about coping with the emotional side effects of variance in Chapter 12, "Avoiding Physical and Emotional Mistakes."

7. Refer back to this book as necessary, as well as to other books on your game.
Nothing beats experience at the tables—but just playing and doing nothing else is worse than not playing, at least for a poker apprentice such as yourself. Most of your low-limit opponents won't spend *any* time away from the table analyzing the game; they just come for the action. That's one of your biggest advantages, so don't forget to use it. Keep dipping back into this book and your other poker books to see what you missed on your first read, and what you can now understand for the first time because you've been there.

Antes, Odds, and Outs: Theory You Can Use

M any poker books for beginners talk about basic poker theory, but few do much to put theory into practice. This chapter is different. You should come away from your reading with a clear idea of how advanced players not only make good poker decisions based on the odds, but manipulate these odds to their advantage. You don't need to know a ton of math to immediately improve your game in this area.

As a simple example, I'll discuss the need to play much tighter than you're used to in a home game. Even as you read these words, you're probably thinking you can skip this topic because you already know all about it—but in my experience, most recreational players making their first ventures onto casino turf often think they're playing tight when in fact they're still leaking chips. My intent is to show you the reasons *why* you have to play so tight and what we really mean by the word.

What theory will do for you

As a seasoned home-game player, you've probably absorbed rules of thumb for deciding whether you should fold, call, bet, or raise in a given situation. As you begin your casino career, you'll initially do much the same, even after developing a sound basic strategy. It'll be a long time before you advance beyond such notions as knowing you want company for speculative drawing hands—but how *much* company?—and only one or two opponents for something solid like a big pair or two pair—but *why* exactly?

Two warnings: First, don't expect this skill to come easily; even once you've learned the rudiments, it will often desert you under pressure. But it will come, especially if you practice as I suggest, and you can eventually make it second nature. Once you gain experience, you can begin thinking less in terms of rules, and more in terms of calculating your odds and outs—two words we'll focus heavily on later in this chapter. Your poker will become more flexible, more adaptive, and more situational. And remember, our goal is to become a situational player, able to take advantage of those players who know only the "rules" and can't consciously alter their behavior as a result.[1]

Second, just because you know the words "odds" and "outs" and can even (miracle of miracles) *count* your literal outs and pot odds, don't expect this to make you a winning player. With the rise in Internet poker and the spate of poker books now available, many young low-limit players are capable of expounding at length about their outs on a given hand and what the pot was offering them. That doesn't mean they're applying this knowledge correctly. For example, outs can be tainted, meaning if your card comes in it may give an opponent a better hand then yours; you rarely hear these talkative types count their *untainted* odds. Nor in their recital of the odds do they talk of effective odds, implied odds, or *reverse* implied odds—even though these things are what you should be making your decisions on, not just the money in the middle by itself.

Strangely enough, the above concepts are what I'm referring to when I say that there are some odds-based improvements to your game that you can make right away, without having to do a lot of math. More on that when we get to it; in the mean-

---

1. For fans of "The Matrix," this should sound familiar. "You think that's air you're breathing?" Learn the underlying poker reality and you can start bending it—at least, that's how it will seem to the uninitiated.

time, bear in mind that anyone who brags at the table about reading Sklansky probably didn't understand a word.

Understanding expectation

First, a warning: these next few pages may get scary, but they're well worth your while.

In Chapter 1, we touched upon the fact that professional poker players are always thinking about whether a given action—a call, fold, check, bet, or raise—will give them what's called *positive expectation.* In other words, will it make or lose them money in the long run?

Let's get more formal here, because this concept of expectation is more important than anything else in poker. Although I've given you a shorthand definition above, expectation is properly a mathematical term, borrowed from that subset of mathematics which deals with probability theory.[2] In its simplest form, expectation can be stated as follows: If you stand to win X dollars if an event occurs that has the probability P, but will win nothing otherwise, your expectation is X times P. Let's say for example that you expect to win a $100 pot half the time. If this is the case, your expectation is 50 percent (expressed as .5) times $100, or $50.

Not making sense? That's where the "long run" part of the concept comes in. If the event in our example occurs just once, you'll win either $100 or nothing—not your expectation of

---

2. It's amusing to realize that probability as a mathematical discipline arose largely because early gamblers wanted to understand why dice or cards behaved as they did. In particular, the Chevalier de Méré in 1654 asked his friend Blaise Pascal, a famous mathematician, to explain why a certain dice wager was losing him money over time; this led to a famous correspondence between Pascal and Pierre de Fermat which answered that question and developed many aspects of probability besides. For more on this subject, see "The Mathematics of Games and Gambling," by Edward Packel.

$50. If it occurs 10 times and you average the 10 results, this average will come closer to $50 than your result for just one event—but most of the time it won't be exactly $50. If the event occurs one *million* times, however, your average result will be so close to $50 that for all intents and purposes you'll have fully realized your expectation.

Applied to poker, expectation gets a little more complicated, since you must now pay a price, in the form of either calling or making a bet, in exchange for your chance of winning. Therefore we adjust our equation to include a cost as well as a reward. An actual formula now becomes useful:

E = (Event A * Probability of A) + (Event B * Probability of B)

This is a general form, but we can turn it into poker terms with a couple of tweaks:

E = (Pot * Probability of winning) - (Bet * Probability of losing)

Let's plug a very simple example into this formula to see how it works. If I can win a $100 pot half the time I play, what's the biggest bet I can afford to call? Well, since in the long run my average win will be $50, it makes sense that the maximum I can afford to lose should also average $50. Plug this into the formula, and we see that if I call a $100 bet each time, I'll be breaking even:

0 = $100 * .5 - $100 * .5

We can put this into words by saying that half the time I'll lose my $100 (averaging a $50 loss), and the other half of the time I'll not only get my bet back, but I'll win the $100 pot as well (averaging a $50 win).

To have positive expectation in this case, any of several factors would have to change. The pot could get bigger, while the bet size stayed the same; or I could win the same size pot, but win it more than half the time; or the bet size could drop to less than $50. Any of these factors gives me a winning bet; likewise, reversing any of these factors gives me a losing bet: for example, if I don't win as big a pot, or if the bet size increases beyond $50, or if I don't win at least half the time.

Here's a more realistic example.[3] Let's say we're head-up on the river, and I'm first to act; I've just bet $10, which you must at least call to have a shot at winning a pot that now totals $100 with my bet added to it. Again, for you to break even would mean your expectation equals zero; in that case our equation would look like:

$$0 = (\$100 * \text{Prob. of winning}) - (\$10 * \text{Prob. of losing})$$

Let's flip the rightmost term over to the other side of the equality sign, so we're working with positive values in both cases:

$$\$10 * \text{Probability of losing} = \$100 * \text{Probability of winning}$$

A few more algebraic judo flips, and we get:

$$\text{Probability of losing} / \text{Probability of winning} = 10$$

Now, any time there are mutually exclusive outcomes, the probabilities involved always add up to equal 100 percent, which we express simply as 1. This lets us express the probability of winning in our example as 10 times the probability of losing, and *that* lets us solve for the probability of losing as follows:

$$\text{Probability of losing} * 10 + \text{Probability of losing} = 1$$

I will spare you the last bit of nasty math here and just tell you that to break even in this case, you need to win a little less than 10 percent of the time—more precisely, 9 1/11 of the time, or 9.0909091 percent. Of course, that's when you only call my bet. If you raise, that changes the equation, since you've now altered the amounts you can lose and win.

---

3. If all these equations are getting to you, feel free to skip ahead. The inferences we draw are what will matter, not the calculations themselves.

The point here is not to have you solving equations in your head at the table—you'd surely drive yourself and everyone else crazy—but to show you that the math *does* matter and is actually the basis for trying to beat poker or any similar game. It's only by repeatedly putting ourselves in situations where our long-term expectation is positive that we hope to make any money.

In practice, poker expectation quickly becomes complicated by non-mathematical factors, and can no longer be cast as a single equation in all but the most simple of cases. To take a straightforward example, we might assume that raising on Third Street in seven-card stud will maximize our expectation if we've been dealt rolled-up Aces; but actually, it will *minimize* our expectation if our raise frightens everyone into folding!

For now, you may find it easier to think of expectation simply as a balancing act: We've got a reward on the one hand and a cost on the other. Is the reward big enough, and will we win it often enough to justify the price we pay all the times we don't win?

Understanding outs and odds, along with pot odds, implied odds, and reverse implied odds

I promised you we'd turn theory into practice, so here's where we start. The formula I just showed you is the mathematical bedrock of expectation. But as useful as it is for research, it's just too complicated to use when you're sitting at the table. Instead, good players make their real-time calculations about expectation using what we call *odds* and *outs*.

Let's begin by defining our terms:

Outs are cards that will help you. If you flop a flush draw in hold'em, for example, you have seen four cards in your suit—the two in your hand and the two on the board—and therefore know that nine cards remain that can make your flush. You have nine outs.

Odds, without further qualification, generally means the chances of making a particular hand. The calculation of odds with more than one card to come requires some extra-fancy math, but for exactly one card to come, it's simply the ratio of the cards that don't help you versus the cards that do. In our hold'em example, there are 47 unseen cards left in the deck; the odds against our making the flush on the turn are the 38 cards that don't help us versus the 9 cards that do, which reduces to about 4 to 1 odds against us.

Pot odds is the ratio of the money in the middle, including any bets now on the table before the action gets to us, to the price we will have to pay to stay in the hand—for example, a single bet if no one has raised and we anticipate no one will raise behind us. You can see now that we prefer to look at our card chances in terms of odds rather than probabilities because it makes it easier to compare card odds to pot odds. In the case of our flush, if the pot is at least four times larger than the bet to us, we would seem to have an easy call.

This is where many recreational players screw up, because they haven't thought beyond what they can count on their fingers to what the true odds might be if they could see their opponents' cards. Let's introduce three more odds-related concepts that will help us cope—one that typically works in our favor, and two that typically work against us, depending on the type of hand we hold.

Implied odds come into effect when there is more than one card to come and you're playing a drawing hand, such as a flush or straight draw. (Keep in mind however that almost any hand that can improve in some way can be considered a drawing hand, such as two pair that can improve to a full house or even trips that can improve to quads, or a big pair that has hopes of making a backdoor flush in hold'em.)

Here's an example of implied odds in hold'em. Say you sneak a look at your cards before the flop and find a pair of fours. Not a powerhouse by itself, but a *set* of fours—now, that would be a hand to conjure with. Assuming no one raises, how much company do you need to profitably limp in with this hand? Strictly speaking, the odds against flopping a set are nearly 8 to 1 against—but in fact, you can call if you're getting just 5 to 1 pot odds—that is, only five other players see the flop with you. How can this be?

First, you're planning to continue with this hand only if you hit your set on the flop; otherwise, you'll fold. That limits the price you're paying to the current bet, usually one small bet, half of what the bet size will be later on. Second, you're figuring that if you *do* hit your set, you'll be the heavy favorite to win, and can therefore discount the cost of any future bets you make. You're hoping these bets will be called by your opponents, but you see them as carrying only a fraction of the usual risk. Put it all together, and you're weighing the price of buying one card now versus your expected total win if you make your big hand. So in this example, while your immediate pot odds to buy the card are 5 to 1, your implied odds are more like 15 to 1. Quite a difference. It's worth noting, however, that when you are wrong about implied odds—such as when you flop a set but someone else flops a bigger set—it almost always costs you a lot of chips.

Reverse implied odds go the other way. Again, they apply only if there is more than one card to go; but now you are holding a hand that will have a hard time improving, such as a pair of Aces in either stud or hold'em, and your opponents are the ones drawing to flushes or straights. You have only two outs to improve to trips, for example, while your opponents have many more outs to make their hands. Against one such opponent, you are a heavy favorite with your made hand versus their unmade hand; but against many drawing opponents, you become a dog. This is the reason you typically raise with a big pair early—to drive out drawing hands, or at the least ruin their implied odds. You'd rather be head-up with a single drawing hand or someone holding a weaker pair hand.

Tainted outs further influence your real odds. They especially apply to hold'em, where a common card that helps you (say, one of your flush cards) can help an opponent more (say, by pairing the board and making a full house for someone with a set). Going back to our hold'em example, if you think you might be up against a set, you must throw out two of your flush outs, giving you only seven untainted outs to work with and thus a significantly worse draw. For you to profitably continue, there must be more money in the pot than with an untainted draw.

A similar concept applies in stud if you hold something like two medium pair on Fifth Street and are up against a probable straight draw and an apparent pair of Kings: You are in danger of being beaten by the straight or by a bigger two pair, and even if you make a full house, there's a chance the Kings will make a bigger full house. Once you get beyond Roy West's rules of thumb, you find yourself deciding whether to play on or fold in such a situation by estimating the likely size of the pot you could win versus the adjusted odds of making your hand but getting beaten by a better hand. If it sounds messy, it is; yet a good stud player must eventually come up with rough-and-ready estimates of this sort.

Practical ways to learn and apply odds and outs

Most of the time you don't need to make fancy calculations in real time: the proper play may be obvious, or the key factors may be more psychological or logical than mathematical. But the more you can calculate or recall previous calculations, the better you can make many decisions that at first seem routine. I'll give some examples in a little while.

The key to making calculations isn't learning how to do fractions or probabilities in your head, but memorizing common scenarios in advance. I like to work on such memorization a little at a time, in between improving other aspects of my game. It's daunting, since remembering figures doesn't come easy for me, but it pays such big dividends I keep chipping away. Here's how I recommend you do it:

First, take a look at the basic odds tables in the back of books like Roy West's or "Hold'em Poker" by David Sklansky. You can just work off the page, if your memory is good, or you can make flash cards and practice that way, if your memory is as bad as mine is. Sure, it's a lot of work to make up a set of flash cards and actually drill yourself, but do you want to win or just pay off other players?

Second, once you have the basic odds half-way memorized, start doing some calculations away from the table. Hold'em is relatively easy; even your odds with two cards to come are available from either the Sklansky hold'em book or Abdul Jalib's Web site.[4] When you analyze a hand you feel you could have played better, go over your outs and odds. Did you really have a call with your straight draw, or did the two-flush on the flop mean that with five opponents you were likely drawing dead—especially after the pot was raised and re-raised ahead of you?

Seven-stud is more complicated to figure, because the exposed cards and the number of players have a big effect on your calculations. You can still work out lots of scenarios ahead of time, however. Here's a simple example: When counting outs on Third Street in a full game, you'll have generally seen 10 cards including your own, leaving 42 cards in the deck. Let's say you've been dealt trip Jacks and suspect an opponent of having a pair of Queens; if both his other Queens are live, he

---

4. See Chapter 13, "Refining Your Game" on page 136.

has two outs to make higher trips, giving him odds of 20 to 1 (40 to 2, divided by 2) to improve to best hand on the next card. If one of his outs is dead because a Queen is someone else's door card, his odds worsen to 41 to 1, a significant difference.

On the later streets in stud, you'll have seen more cards, so you adjust your calculations accordingly. In a typical loose low-limit game there will generally be about 38 cards left in the deck on Fourth Street, 35 on Fifth Street, and 32 on Sixth Street. Let's say you had a medium two-pair on Sixth Street and needed to fill up to beat a bigger two-pair, and all your pair cards were live: this would give you four outs, for odds of 7 to 1 against (28 to 4, divided by 4). This of course doesn't take into account your opponent's chances of also filling up. You can take the exercise further and figure out how often he will fill up too, then calculate how big a pot you need to call in various betting scenarios. It may seem like a lot of trouble, but once you get to thinking about various big hands you've won or lost, you'll find yourself wondering what the real answer is. That's when you sit down to work it out.

The next step in practicing is to start calculating odds and outs at the table. Start counting the pot size when you're not in a hand. Calculate the odds for each player to call—notice how they keep improving the later a player's position—and if someone raises, do a quick calculation of how this shortens the odds for anyone who has not yet come in. Once you're decent at this, it's only a short step to making such calculations for yourself when you're in the hand. And don't forget to consider tainted outs, implied odds, and reverse implied odds!

Odds and outs in action

Here are two examples of how understanding pot odds can help you determine if your hand is playable after the flop, or if you should pass and wait for a better opportunity. They're both pretty detailed, so read them through a couple of times if necessary. If you still don't get it, move on, but make a note to revisit this section of the book when your game has improved.

Example one: You're on the button in a nine-handed $10/$20 hold'em game, and look down to find you've been dealt A9s[5] in spades—a raising hand if you're opening the pot in the cut-off or on the button. However, in this case, a middle-position player opens the pot by limping in; two other limpers follow him, and you decide to play your hand for its drawing value, meaning you call rather than raise. The small blind calls after you, the big blind checks, and you get to see the flop six-handed without a raise. There's $60 in the middle of the table at this point.[6]

The flop comes Ks 8s 3c, and you try to maintain composure as you realize you've flopped the nut flush draw. Both blinds check, and the first limper bets $10. He's called by the next two players. The action is to you now: should you call, fold, or raise?

Obviously you know from experience that it's worth at least a call—but let's put aside our assumptions and our experience for a moment, and do the math. To start with, there's now $90 in the pot. Assuming that neither of the blinds raises after you, it'll cost you $10 to see the turn, meaning the pot is offering you 9-to-1 odds. You've memorized your outs and odds for hold'em, so you know you're a little bit better than 2-to-1 to make your hand by the river. Compare the pot odds to your

---

5. A word about hold'em hand notation: A hand such as King-Queen suited is written KQs; King-Queen unsuited is written KQ or sometimes KQo; a Ten is written T, so that for example pocket Tens would be TT and Ten-Nine would be T9; and a small card is often written x—for example, a suited Ace with a Deuce through Five would be written Axs, emphasizing the nature of the hand rather than the exact value of the second card.

6. You're right! The pot would be a little less than $60 because of the rake. However, we'll disregard the rake in this first example to keep things simple. It becomes more significant in our second example, as you'll see.

drawing odds, and you can see that you have huge positive expectation for a call.

However, you should also consider *raising* here. Let's do the math for this scenario as well. If you raise, one or both of the blinds will probably fold, which you don't like—but they may be planning to fold anyway to just the single bet. Meanwhile the three players in front of you have already invested $10 each in this flop, so it's a cinch they'll call your raise too. You'd be getting 3-to-1 odds on your raise in a situation where you're a 2-to-1 dog—once again giving you positive expectation on your investment. Your only worry would be that the original flop bettor might reraise, knocking out the two players after him and getting the two of you heads-up. That would increase your price, cut down your implied odds, and in general make raising here a mistake.

To decide, you need additional information: Are the blinds holding chips in their hands behind you, indicating they're ready to call? In that case, you may just want to call also, keeping them in. If on the other hand they look like they want to fold to the single bet, you'll need to consider the initial flop bettor: Is he an aggressive player who might reraise here, or is he a fairly passive, predictable player who will be intimidated by your raise? If it's the latter, then a raise may well be your best option. Keep in mind that with your position on the button, a raise may have the additional advantage of buying you a free turn card, allowing you to see the river more cheaply should the turn not help.

We're not done yet—there's one more reason you might want to raise. This has to do with the fact that your hand has more potential outs than just your flush draw. Consider that if an Ace falls on the turn or river, your pair of Aces with a Nine kicker may have a shot at beating the current bettor's presumed pair of Kings. Remember, no one raised preflop, making it unlikely that anyone limped a crushing top-pair hand like AK (you must know your players to make this evaluation). That being the case, a raise could conceivably knock out tight players holding hands like AJ or AT, giving you as many as three additional outs. You'd then be only a 1.5-to-1 dog to make a pair of Aces or better by the river. In this case, you decide that if a better Ace *is* out there, it's most likely to be found among the three players who've already called. You can't knock them out, so you're better off just calling. You put your chips in, and as you expected, both blinds muck. Four players remain to see the turn card.

The dealer burns and turns the Six of diamonds, a blank for you but probably for everyone else too. The first player bets again, $20 this time, and again gets a call from the second player. Alas, the third player folds, hurting not only your pot odds but your implied odds, since he won't be around on the river to call you if you make a hand. Even so the pot is now offering you $140 to $20, or 7-to-1 odds to draw to your flush. Since your odds of making your flush with one card to come are roughly 4-to-1, your expectation for calling is still positive. You throw your chips in and hold your breath waiting for the river card.

And here we must leave you. You've played well, and you can be confident that all your decisions thus far have had positive expectation, no matter what the river brings.

Example two: Your hand will be similar, but we'll change the number of opponents. This will have the effect of changing the pot odds you'll be getting as well. Let's say it's the same $10/$20 hold'em game, but this time you're in the big blind holding J6s of spades. A middle player limps, the small blind folds, leaving his $5 in the middle, and you check. You and the middle player see the flop heads-up with only $25 in the pot.

The flop again comes Ks 8s 3c, so you again have a flush draw, though not the nuts in this case. In some cases it would be correct to aggressively bet your draw here—a play called a semi-bluff—but your opponent stiffens slightly at the sight of the flop, causing you to opt for caution and check. He bets $10.

You pause and remind yourself to do the math. There's $35 in the pot, and a call will cost you $10 to chase your flush draw— in other words, you're getting 3.5-to-1 odds. You remember that your odds of making the flush by the river haven't changed: they're still about 2-to-1, giving you what you think is an easy call. You put your chips forward confidently. If David Sklansky could see you, he'd be frowning, but you're not thinking about Sklansky just now.

The turn fails to make your flush. You check, your opponent bets. You consider your options. With $65 in the pot and a $20 price to call, the pot is now laying you 3.25-to-1. Suddenly you realize that you have only one card left to draw to, and that the odds for making your flush with one card are only about 4-to-1. Comparing pot odds to drawing odds, you see your expectation has abruptly turned negative. Without hesitation, you fold your hand.

Now our imaginary Sklansky wouldn't just frown, he'd grimace! The reason he'd find your play so objectionable is that you're not thinking about the odds deeply enough here. Your expectation for this hand can be either positive or negative—it all depends on your opponent and how he'll play the river. Without that knowledge, you probably shouldn't even have called the flop bet.

Here's how we can calculate this: We know that the price for calling your opponent's flop and turn bets combined is exactly $30. If your flush comes in on the river, we must now consider two scenarios. In the first, you check, planning to check-raise—but your opponent checks behind you! In this case, if we add up your profit, you make only $65. That means your *effective odds*, as Sklansky calls this kind of lump-sum calculation, would have been slightly better than 2-to-1—but only if there were no rake. In many cases, the rake may be big enough to crush your effective odds, dropping them to *less* than 2-to-1. And since your odds of making the flush are also slightly less than 2-to-1, your play here is very marginal. Add in the small chance that one or more of your outs may not be clean—for example, if your opponent has flopped a hand like two pair or a set and is drawing to a full house—and your expectation becomes dubious at best. Hence you are better off folding on the flop.

In the second scenario, however, your opponent is prone to giving action: if you check the river when your flush card comes in, not only will he bet, but he'll call your check-raise. If that's the case, you now win $105, meaning your effective odds are about 3-to-1—easily enough to justify seeing both the turn and river at 2-to-1 drawing odds. It's true there's still a slim chance of getting counterfeited by a flush card that makes your opponent a full house, but since that's not very likely, you can assume you have positive expectation here.

Our third example is much simpler, yet just as important; it's a test of sorts, one that many low-limit players fail. Again, we're talking hold'em. Let's say you've raised preflop with a big pair against a horde of loose-passive players; now the flop comes with both a middle straight draw and a flush draw to which you have no claim, neither of your pair cards being the right color. What do you do? I often see players jam the pot with their big pair in this situation, or else call raises and reraises to the bitter end; and yet in many cases a fold on the flop is the best play. It's a clear case of reverse implied odds. The same thing applies in a loose stud game when you raise on Third Street with wired Aces, but get several callers. If by Fifth Street you haven't improved your one big pair, and several opponents are showing strong flush and straight boards, you're better off folding your bullets rather than persisting in a losing cause.

Reviewing these three examples, we can see that they demonstrate several points:

- Whether it's stud or hold'em, you prefer many opponents for starting hands that are pure draws, such as straights and flushes. This provides positive expectation—not only because of the immediate pot odds, but because of the implied odds of having more opponents available on the expensive streets to give you action, should you get lucky and make your hand.

- Since you can't always count on a single opponent giving you a lot of action on later streets, it's rarely wise to chase draws head-up on an early street without any other value. The pot can't get big enough to justify chasing.

- Conversely, hands that can't easily improve, such as a big pair or even a big two-pair, prefer to avoid reverse implied odds by getting head-up or three-way. This is as true in stud as it is in hold'em. (Of course, when these hands *do* improve, they become monsters and you don't mind a crowd chasing you.)

- Calculating your odds may seem simple at first, but it quickly gets more complicated once you start considering *all* your outs and all the possible betting scenarios. When you're just starting out, this might be too much to think about in the middle of a hand, but as you get more comfortable with odds and outs, you can begin to use your knowledge to increase your expectation—for example, by raising in key spots to knock out hands which otherwise might draw out on you. Our example showed how you might do this in hold'em, but you can make a similar play in stud.

Odds and outs in a home game

If your home game is like mine, it's super-loose on all streets, with many players staying in and getting hooked despite all manner of raises. This being the case, it makes sense to play primarily drawing hands, especially draws that could make monsters. Why? Because your implied odds are enormous. Meanwhile, you stay away from good but not great hands that don't have the potential to improve, because of the reverse implied odds these hands carry in the same situation.

You can go still further and do what at first seems counter-intuitive: bet and even raise aggressively on the early streets with a pure drawing hand, as long as it has a chance to make the nuts or close to it. This especially applies to high-low games with a hand that has the potential to scoop. With so many players, your bets or raises are close enough to neutral that you aren't doing your implied odds serious damage; and because you will often be folding early if you don't improve your draw on the next street or two, your buddies will be fully willing to call your maximum bets and raises when you *do* make your monster hand. They'll think you're a wild and crazy player who gets lucky a lot, rather than a calculating machine.

Understanding the ante, the rake, and the betting structure

Now that you know about expectation, you're ready to understand how it applies to underpinnings of an individual poker game—the ante, the rake, and the betting structure. These three topics are rarely dealt with by bad beginners' books, but they're essential in deciding strategy whenever you sit down to play. True, there is no rake in a home game, but an understanding of the ante and the betting structure is still crucial to proper play—even if most home game players are blithely unaware of it.

The ante: it equals action

Why do we put money in the middle of the table before we deal the cards? Intuitively we know it's to get more action going. This is perfectly illustrated by that perverse little number sometimes called in dealer's choice home games: five-card draw, Jacks-or-better progressive. Everyone antes and it's Jacks or better to open; if no one can open, everyone antes again and now it's Kings or better; if the same happens, then everyone antes a third time and now it's Aces to open!

The pot has grown so big by now with all those antes in it that even if someone now opens, meaning they have Aces or better, you're justified in playing a much weaker hand than normal—basically anything that might draw out and beat a pair of unimproved Aces. In terms of expectation, we can afford to lose more often, even though we don't win any more often—the bigger reward compensates.

Conversely, if the ante is small or non-existent, the risk now looms above the initial reward for most hands and you should be quite choosy. This should be obvious—yet the first time you sit down in a no-ante, $1-$3 or $1-$5 spread limit stud game, you'll discover it's not at all obvious to many of your fellow gamblers. The only money at issue is the $1 forced bet, or bring-in, contributed by the low card showing. This being the case, it's crazy for an underpair like Jacks to chase a probable overpair like Kings—and yet recreational stud players do this all the time. This turns no-ante stud into a game of trapping, in which you patiently play only very good hands and collect donations from anyone chasing you. In Las Vegas, some no-ante stud tables can get so tight you're reduced to always limping with your big pairs, in hopes of persuading someone to join you.

What's the overriding lesson here? The larger the ante or blinds compared to the bet size—commonly called an over-ante—the more starting hands you are justified in playing; and the smaller the ante or blinds, the more you should tighten up. Indeed, in games with over-antes, good players will start raising on the opening street with much weaker cards than usual, hoping to steal the antes, since that is now a profitable play.

Every time you sit down to play in a game, then, you should weigh the size of the antes and adjust accordingly. Don't forget this if you're visiting someone else's home game where the ante is a dollar and the opening bet is limited to a maximum of two dollars—an *enormous* over-ante—or if you're considering sitting down at the casino in a $1-$5 stud game with a .50 cent ante, also big if not quite as humongous. Of course, in the situation at the casino, you'll also need to consider the *rake*.

The rake: as cruel as its name

Casinos and clubs must make money from poker players—at least enough to defray expenses—and therefore they either charge you time for your seat, or take a percentage of the pot. The latter is called the rake. The terrible truth is that at the lower limits, the rake can be as large as 10 percent, enough to make it hard to beat the game even if your opponents are very bad and very loose. If the ante is small this is less of a problem because you just tighten up and play only hands with a high probability of winning. But if the ante is big, as it is in that $1-$5 stud game mentioned above, now you are stuck: if you play too tight you'll be throwing your money away in antes, but if you play too loose you're throwing it away in the direction of the slot in the table by the side of the dealer. What to do? If the opposition is especially loose and bad, you will be okay, but you are not happy with the situation.

The answer here is to move up as soon as you feasibly can to a higher limit where the rake percentage becomes smaller. For example, if you have a choice between $2/$4 hold'em and $3/$6 hold'em, you are almost always better off opting for the latter, because the rake in dollars is typically the same in both cases, but the percentage is smaller at $3/$6. And note that in hold'em, the point at which the rake takes effect has a big effect on late-position strategy: if the equivalent of the big blind is taken off the table as soon as the flop comes, trying to steal the blinds with a late raise becomes a negative proposition with anything but a very good hand—and if you have a very good hand, you want to earn more than just the blinds anyway.

When you're just starting out, a good exercise to remind yourself of all this is to ask what the rake is before sitting down to play. Often it's posted at the table on a placard, but the dealer will always know.

The betting structure: how cheap can you buy, how dear can you sell?

What we call "structure" is really a combination of the ante, the initial bet size on earlier streets, and the bet size on later streets. In fixed-limit poker, for example $5/$10 stud or hold'em, the bet is $5 on Third and Fourth streets and it doubles to $10 on Fifth Street. In spread-limit, pot-limit, and no-limit poker, the amount that can be bet is more flexible. In spread-limit, such as $1-$5 stud, your opening bet on any street can be the minimum or the maximum or anything in-between. In pot-limit, you can bet or raise the size of the pot, which creates big leverage for bluffs. And in no-limit, you can bet your entire stack of thousands of dollars on the first card or as little as a one-dollar chip on the last card.

All of this affects what we'll talk about when we get to the subject of implied odds—namely, how cheaply can you get in with a speculative hand, and how much will you be able to extort from opponents if you actually make that hand? If you're holding a couple of small suited connectors in no-limit hold'em that you've limped in with before the flop in hopes of making a killing, but Doyle Brunson abruptly moves in on you with his entire stack, your plan has been spoiled and you will have to fold even if he might be bluffing. Likewise in $1-$5 stud, you have the option of raising the puny $1 bring-in with the maximum hammer of $5 in hopes of thinning the field and improving the chances of your pair of Aces holding up.

In a fixed-limit game, the inability to bet the moon on later streets means you must be very careful about your odds early on. For example, if your $3/$6 hold'em game is constantly being jammed before the flop by loose-aggressive types, the double bet on the later streets will *never* be big enough to make a hand like medium suited connectors profitable. As I say, we'll talk more about this later under the subject of implied odds.

Understanding the structure will help you away from the casino also, if you happen to run into a home game where the limit never increases—say, where you can only bet or raise a dollar on any street. I have a buddy who plays in such a game and does well, but he understands his profit comes from loose players drawing dead to his monster hands and monster draws, not from any notions of knocking opponents out. See also our earlier discussion about applying odds and outs to playing in a home game.

Playing tight: how tight is tight enough?

My favorite example of the need to play tighter than you might think necessary is from $1-$3 no-ante seven-card stud. Novice stud players at this limit love to limp in with small or medium pocket pairs whenever they can, even if they have only a small doorcard. They reason that if they can get in cheaply on Third Street, they'll make a handsome payoff if they get lucky and trip up on Fourth Street. They congratulate themselves on being smart enough not to get involved if they make a death hand like two small pair instead. Of *course* they're playing tight!

If these smart players paused to actually do the math, however, they'd realize that the $1 price of limping in, the small $3 maximum bet, and the precise odds against hitting trips combine to make this play unprofitable without at least five or more loose, passive limpers for company. Even then it's marginal, because small trips may well need to fill up to win against a whole table of loose opponents. Therefore, hands like these should routinely be thrown away at this limit.[7]

You should also be getting the idea that "tight" means more than just observing a rigid hierarchy of starting hand requirements—it means situationally tight! If you've got split Jacks on 3rd street in low-limit seven-stud and a rock raises with an Ace as his doorcard, you fold, because it's a losing play to chase an overpair in a small-ante game. Or if you've got AK before the flop in hold'em, you fold behind a tight raiser who've you watched only raise with QQ or better rather than trap yourself with a dominated hand.

A final reason to learn how to play painfully tight is variance. As I've mentioned, you can go through streaks that last hours, days, and yes, even *weeks*, wherein you get very few or no playable hands; or where you get hands that consistently come in second-best. If you don't know how to tighten up during periods of bad cards, you will leak back all the money you made during your periods of good cards, and then some. One of the hardest skills to master in poker is the ability to play well despite running bad, and in fact, most recreational players never do master it. I'll talk more about conquering this demon in Chapter 12, "Avoiding Physical and Emotional Mistakes," but until then, work on developing the ability to tighten up at will. That's the first and most important step.

---

7. Note that if you're playing $1-$5 no-ante stud rather than $1-$3, the play now becomes profitable because the bet size has increased. See Chapter 13, "Refining Your Game" on page 136, for more on this.

Chapter 5

Who to Study for Basic Strategy— and Who Not To

A s I mentioned in Chapter 1, poker books tend to fall into three categories: advanced, beginner, and garbage. Unfortunately the garbage books far outnumber the good ones, and if you're just starting to get serious about poker, it can be hard at first glance to tell the difference. And bad advice can cost you a lot more than the price listed on the jacket cover.

Having read virtually every poker book there is, I'll spare you the time, money, and aggravation. This chapter contains my recommendations for the top beginner books on whatever form of casino poker you've chosen to master. Since even good books have their share of flaws and omissions, I'll point these out and recommend additional sources of information as necessary.

One side note: You won't find a list here of books specifically to avoid. It would be a long list indeed, but some of the authors are well-known in the poker world, and getting them mad wouldn't serve any good purpose. Just keep in mind that if I don't recommend a book here or in Chapter 5, "Refining Your Game," you're taking your chances.[1]

---

1. If you want to read some scathing reviews of bad poker books, check out Mason Malmuth's book "Gambling Theory and Other Topics." He tends to be dead on in his assessments and can be quite funny. One warning: He pans the first edition of Lee Jones's hold'em book (one of the books I'm going to recommend to you) but has since written a favorable review of the second edition.

Books on seven-card stud

There are exactly two books, no more and no less, that you absolutely must read if your game is seven-card stud:

"7 Card Stud: The Complete Course in Winning at Medium and Lower Limits," by Roy West

As I said in Chapter 1, this is the book that saved my own poker career. There is no beginner book about any form of poker that will teach you more about studying your opponent as the key to success. I'd recommend reading West even if you want to play hold'em—he will get you thinking about how to apply the same process of reading hands to hold'em. And it's a very short book, so you won't need to invest a lot of time.

West does a solid job of presenting basic stud strategy; if you play as he recommends, you'll do fine in $1-$3 and $1-$5 spread limit, and probably do okay in $5-$10 and $10-$20 fixed limit as well.[2] However, you'll eventually run into situations he doesn't talk enough about, such as how to vary your play to handle different types of games—for example, loose-aggressive tables where many players are jamming the pot on the thinnest of margins, versus loose-passive games where there are just as many callers to the river but hardly any raising on the early streets. Therefore, once you've played enough to get most of the classic beginner's mistakes out of your system—like not playing tight enough or playing dead cards—I recommend you tackle one additional book. This book has an intimidating title:

---

2. As we'll discuss further in Chapter 9, there's a huge structural difference between "little stud" games like $1-$3 no-ante and the "big stud" games which start at $5-$10. West talks about this difference to some extent, but not as much as I'd like.

"Seven Card Stud for Advanced Players," by David Sklan-sky, Mason Malmuth, and Ray Zee

Like other books by Sklansky and Malmuth writing in tandem, "Seven Card Stud for Advanced Players" (SCSAP) is a tough read. Neither Sklansky nor Malmuth claims to be a prose stylist, and the book suffers from poor organization. But don't let this stop you: if you persevere with SCSAP you'll pick up ideas you won't find anywhere else. For example, you'll learn about raising with the third-best hand in a multi-way pot on fifth street to knock out the second-best hand and thus improve your overall chances of winning the pot. It sounds crazy until you understand the logic behind it.

Keep in mind, however, that SCSAP is really meant for bigger games than $1-$5 or $5-$10—specifically, it was written for $15-$30 to $30-$60 games. The moves you learn from it must be applied with caution, and never against weak players who will stubbornly call you down no matter what you represent. Most of the time you're going to be playing as Roy West recommends—solid, not fancy.

These are the only two books I absolutely recommend for seven-card stud. I'll suggest some optional further reading in Chapter 13, "Refining Your Game," but for now you're all set.

Books on hold'em

There is no single book that covers beginning hold'em as completely and well as Roy West covers stud. Possibly this is because hold'em is initially counter-intuitive compared to stud, even though both games become equally tough as you move up in limit. At any rate, I'm going to recommend two books to start with, each of which complements the other.

"Winning Low-Limit Hold'em," by Lee Jones

Like me, Lee Jones is an amateur poker player. Amateur or not, he broke new ground when ConJelCo published his first edition of "Winning Low Limit Hold'em" in 1994: there was no book quite like it on the market. When I was still just a home game player I remember being overwhelmed by Jones's discussion of topics like implicit collusion and implied odds. In fact, I was *so* overwhelmed, I decided not to learn hold'em! (Obviously I changed my mind later on.)

The book is an excellent beginner's primer, but it's not all-inclusive. For one thing, Jones's advice is primarily directed at loose games where many players are contesting most pots. It's true that low-limit games are more often looser than not—but they can also be relatively tight, probably more so the further you get from Las Vegas and California. The $3/$6 afternoon games at the now defunct Mohegan Sun poker room in Connecticut, for example, used to be largely populated by retirees who kept a tight grip on their chips and were reluctant to enter a pot even if someone had limped ahead of them. The result was that a significant number of hands were played four-way, three-way, or head-up.[3]

This is a corner of the map that Jones hasn't filled in. He says you can't bluff at low-limit hold'em—but he's talking about multi-way pots. If you're facing just one or two opponents on the flop, you've got to be able to read when either or both of them are weak and willing to fold to a bet.[4] In effect, you're bluffing, or more likely semi-bluffing with outs if you're called. Granted it's not first on the agenda for the raw beginner, but

---

3. Some writers say "heads-up," others say "head-up." Either way, it means two players going at each other with no one else in the pot.

4. For more on this topic, see "Improve Your Poker," by Bob Ciaffone, and "Middle Limit Hold'em Poker," by Ciaffone and Jim Brier. Both books are on my recommended list in Chapter 13, "Refining Your Game" on page 136.

fairly soon in your hold'em career you need to develop your these sorts of skills just to keep even.

The other area where Jones abbreviates is on reading hands and reading players. He makes good initial suggestions, to which you should pay close attention—but he doesn't go into detail, most likely because he's trying to explain a very complicated game in relatively few pages. That's one of the reasons I've written a complete chapter on this extremely important topic.

Where Jones excels is in working through all the basic multiway scenarios and how to handle them—top pair on the flop, a flush draw versus a paired board, and so on. Overall he does a better job of talking at a beginner's level of understanding than any other hold'em writer, perhaps because he considers himself a student rather than a master. He has been criticized for being too basic, but basic is where you have to start.

"Hold'em Poker," by David Sklansky

This is the other book I recommend you pick up right away, to supplement Lee Jones. It may seem like an odd choice, being as dated as it is: it was first written in 1976, when hold'em was less popular and the blind structure was significantly different than in today's game. It's been revised to keep up with the new blind structure, however. Beyond that, what Sklansky has to say is so mind-blowing that you're short-changing yourself if you don't read him. It's a very short book, but certain sections—for example, "Flops You Want"—will take you a long time to digest. His advice on reading hands is also worth studying, even though it's meant to apply to tougher games than those you'll initially be playing in.

These two books will give you plenty to start with. When you're ready for more, check out the additional reading listed in Chapter 13. Some of it will be too advanced at first, but once you've worked through the sections 2 and 3 of this book, it will start to make sense and be fun besides.

Books on high-low poker

If you feel that despite my warnings you simply must start out your casino career with either Omaha high-low or stud high-low, what books are available for you? Darn few. They are as follows:

"High-Low-Split Poker For Advanced Players," by Ray Zee.

This book covers both high-low stud and high-low Omaha. Zee is no more a natural writer than his fellow Two Plus Two authors Mason Malmuth and David Sklansky, but he's more down-to-earth. His major failing is that he often resorts to pet phrases which amount to code—for example, saying about a particular situation that "you must play poker well" without explaining what the heck he means by that. Other than that, his prescriptions for both games should be memorized. He does a good job of distinguishing between loose low-limit games, where you'll probably be starting out, and tougher, higher-limit games.

"Super/System," by Doyle Brunson and contributors.

This book is now available in paperback and makes a fun read even if you're never going to play Brunson's specialty, no-limit hold'em. It also has an excellent but dated chapter on high-low seven-stud by Brunson in collaboration with the then-youthful David Sklansky. The reason it's dated is that these days, high-low stud is played with a qualifier for low hands (you must have an eight-or-better low), whereas back then there was no qualifier. The chapter is still worth reading for entertainment and to improve your conceptual grasp of high-low poker in general.

"Omaha Hold'em Poker" by Bob Ciaffone.

This is one of the few poker books I don't own—it focuses primarily on high-only Omaha, and I don't play that game very often. I've read through it, however, and Ciaffone's advice seems as sound as ever; moreover, he's widely acknowledged to be an outstanding Omaha player. And with so little available on the high-low split form of the game, the book's one chapter on that topic is probably worth the cover price.

That's it. Now you know who to read to learn your game; get cracking so you can catch up with me as we start Section 2, where we launch ourselves off the basic platform of these books into the realms of advanced poker.

SECTION 2

Playing
the
Other Players

Chapter 6

Your Most Important Poker Weapon

I t was January in Las Vegas, and while the weather outside was uneasy, with an uncomfortable dry chill in the air, the atmosphere inside the poker room of the Mandalay Bay casino was perfect: lots of tourists, me included, and lots of low-limit action.

We had a full ring game going in $1-$5 no-ante stud. Directly across the table from me was a young man in a red warm-up jacket with quite a few piles of loosely stacked chips in front of him. His demeanor was quiet, but his play was relatively aggressive, with lots of betting and an occasional raise. I began watching both him and the cards he showed down. At first he seemed like a good player, because he was winning with good hands. When he started catching cards that weren't as good, I kept watching. I soon discovered he would bet on just about anything. In fact, he would bet if he was high card showing and everyone checked to him, regardless of whether he had a hand or not.

I also discovered he had a tell: when he caught a card that helped him, he would smile a very small, rueful smile—an expression so brief I doubt anyone noticed but me. Unlike everyone else, I was watching faces and not cards during the deal.

Several hands later I was dealt split Queens; my friend across the table had an eight for his door card. On fourth street I tripped up, pairing my door card. He paired his door card too. Seeing him smile when his card came, I knew he'd made trips too—so I checked. He bet the maximum, I raised the maximum, and he stopped smiling. On the next card I caught my full house and wound up beating his smaller full house. Another tourist at the table, impressed by the check-raise, felt obliged to utter this cliché to my opponent: "Man, he played you like a Stradivarius."

The value of reading hands

Actually, despite the onlooker's comment, my play wasn't in any way expert. The point to this anecdote is that back when I was a novice, I would have bet out with my trips rather than check-raise, not having studied my opponent enough to read his hand and know how he'd play it if I checked. Same thing if I were an average or weak low-limit player, or if I'd only read typical poker books for beginners. By playing the hand as I did, I won an extra bet with my check raise. Such extra bets can add up at the end of the night to the difference between winning and losing.

What is reading hands? It's a process of observation and reasoning, the goal of which is to know what cards your opponent is holding, just as if he were playing them face up. David Sklansky has gone so far as to call it "the most important weapon a poker player can have." He's writing about tough games at high limits, but reading hands can be a weapon at low limits as well. More to the point, it's a weapon you've got to master if you want to survive, let alone prosper: As I've already stated, it's my opinion that you can't break even at public poker if you don't have at least a minimal degree of skill in this area. And winning is *definitely* predicated on developing this skill as much as you can, along with refining your game in other areas.

Occasionally a poker book will tell you that reading players doesn't work at the low limits, supposedly because opponents at this level will play almost every hand they're dealt. This is wrong. Even weak opponents who play too many hands still have habits and preferences; you just have to figure out what those are. It is true, however, that it can be easier to read a decent player than an awful player.

An additional bonus to studying your opponents is that it not only helps you read a player's hands, but gives you an edge in predicting how he'll *play* those hands. I'm merging the concepts of reading hands and reading players in this chapter because they go together so logically. In a sense, they're almost the same thing.

Reading hands—the process

The first step in learning how to read hands is learning how to gauge your opponents' starting hands—the first three cards in seven stud, for example, or the first two cards in hold'em. This allows you to narrow down the possibilities for his hand in subsequent rounds, especially in games with exposed cards, whether a community board as in hold'em or individual boards as in stud.

You read starting hands by noting how your opponent prefers to play (or not play) different types of hands under different circumstances: for example, if he'll play small or medium pairs with no other value in seven stud; if he likes to raise versus slowplay certain types of hands, such as small rolled-up trips in seven stud; if he prefers to limp-reraise with hands such as AKs in hold'em; if he is a steady decent player who will never open with certain hands when out of position, such as T9s under the gun in hold'em; and so on and so forth. Obviously such information isn't always *easy* to come by, since you won't often see an opponent show down his hand on the river—but each time you *do* see his cards and put them together with how he played them, you've got yourself a bona fide clue. Accumulate enough clues and you can begin to make accurate guesses at his starting hands. It's as simple as that.

You've also got to observe how your opponent plays various types of hands as they develop on the later streets. These are the specifics that translate into the more overall judgement of whether a player is aggressive or passive, loose or tight. For example, if the game is seven stud, some low-limit players are so excessively timid they'll only bet trips or better, and sometimes not even then if they're looking at a scary board across the table. Meanwhile, other players are so blindly aggressive they'll bet and raise an unimproved pair of Aces on Fifth and Sixth streets into three or four opponents. Some players will bluff-raise the flop in hold'em, but never bluff the turn or river; some never bluff at all, even when they should. Knowing this sort of thing about each of your opponents can help you save or win many extra bets each session.

Another factor is how much your opponent knows about poker. A knowledgeable player will probably place about the right value on his hand, but a weak player may overvalue certain hands (like the player with the Aces in the paragraph above) and bet them heavily in the wrong spot. You need to know who's savvy and who's not, so you can assign the appropriate degree of credibility to their actions. This is part of trying to think like your opponent as much as possible.

Thinking like your opponent leads to another tool for reading hands—the use of deduction, generally on later streets and in games with exposed cards. David Sklansky gives a wonderfully clear example of this in "The Theory of Poker": you have trip Sevens on the river in seven stud, with three players acting ahead of you. First, an open pair of Aces bets; he is called by an open pair of Kings, and called again by an open pair of Queens. Assuming all the players involved are decent, you must assume the showing pair of Kings has at least Kings-up, since he would need that much to beat Aces; you must then assume the pair of Queens has three Queens or better, since he would need that much to beat Kings-up. Your three Sevens are therefore no good and you should fold. Note that the picture would change if the player with the Queens was clueless; now you might have a marginal call, depending on the size of the pot.

Finally, a powerful additional source of information is tells. Tells can be generic—such as when one of your opponents in high-low stud focuses his eyes only on the two low hands facing him across the table, meaning he's probably going low. But the best tells are highly individual, such as a player who nervously bounces his leg under the table when he has a big hand.

Here's another interesting gap in the poker literature: most books, even Mike Caro's remarkable "Book of Tells," don't talk enough about when a tell is useful versus when it's not. Aside from tells that indicate a complete bluff, most giveaways that you'll see in low limit poker are meaningless—*unless* you can put them into the context of what hand a player might be holding and how it relates to your hand. Then the tell can be the difference between winning and losing several bets, or even the entire pot.

In theory, reading tells can get tricky if you're up against a good professional who will deliberately fake a tell to throw you off—but at the lower limits, this rarely happens. Most low-limit players I've come across in public cardrooms are oblivious to the fact that their faces, eyes, and gestures are helping to give away their hands. I'll cover tells in their entirety in Chapter 10.

General tips on analyzing opponents

Later in this section we'll address the specifics of reading hands in hold'em and stud. Before we get to that, here are some general suggestions, comments, and techniques for studying your opponent regardless of game type.

1. You'll get better at "modeling" opponents with practice

Players, especially at the low limits, tend to fall into one or another of several types. Some of these types are so common poker slang has come up with names for them, such as rock or maniac. When you're just starting out, you might have to watch an opponent for an hour before you decide he's a rock. With experience, you may be able to place him in that category with just one or two quick observations, because you now have a more complete model in your head as to how a typical rock plays. (We'll go over all of these common types in Chapter 7, "Labeling your Opponents.")

2. Focus on how opponents' strategies differ from yours

This is especially helpful when you're learning a new game. First, think about how your basic strategy tells you to play certain types of hands, and then see if your opponents deviate from this strategy. For example, in hold'em, most good players prefer to raise with hands like AK or QQ in early position. In low-limit hold'em, however, you'll often find opponents who limp with these same hands (that is, come in without a raise) no matter *what* their position. Immediately you've noted a marker that's easy for you to remember and that can make a significant difference in how you play against these opponents after the flop.

3. Know when to watch

It's best to study opponents when you're not in a hand and can focus without emotion or distractions. You should get plenty of opportunities, because if you're playing properly, you'll be folding a lot. Studying your opponents is a good way to keep yourself in the game despite all these boring folds.

4. Try to guess hands right from the beginning

This is extremely important: Don't wait until opponents reveal their cards on the river to think about how they played them; instead, start trying to read their hands *as soon as the cards are dealt*. Do your best to guess what each might be holding, based on their initial checks, bets, and raises, as well as on their position, their upcards, and what you know about them so far. You'll often have no clue at all, but that's less important than making the effort.

As more cards are dealt and more information becomes available, refine your predictions. If you think a player is on a draw, ask yourself if he's getting the right odds; likewise, if he seems to have a big hand early on, think about how he's playing it compared to the way you would play it, or if he could play it better. Keep counting the pot, too.

Assuming the hand reaches showdown, see if you were right or wrong in your guesses. If you're wrong, work backwards in your mind to see if you missed any clues. Then store away any information you've gained, and settle in to watch the next hand.

As you gain skill and confidence, you'll be able to manage this process while you're playing a hand and not just watching. Your reads will pay off in the form of bets saved and bets won, and you'll start to feel like you're controlling easily readable opponents. Until then, keep working at it. Make it a game within the game.

5. Tricks for keeping track

It's hard to maintain concentration for many hours in a row. It's also hard to remember all the small nuggets of information you pick up about your opponents, especially as new players come in and old ones leave. If you forget what you learned about an opponent, you might as well never have learned it.

One trick I use is to periodically sum up in my head what I've observed about each player, going around the table in order. Another is to walk away from the table and jot notes, again going around the table to make sure to include everyone; if you play with the same players repeatedly at a club or casino, these quick notes can become the basis of a more permanent record.[1] (This technique also has the advantage of forcing you

---

1. As we've already discussed, online venues like Paradise Poker include a Notes feature for just this purpose.

to take a break on a regular basis to keep fresh.) A third trick is to take the specifics you've observed, however small, and generalize from them, describing each player's overall style in terms of loose versus tight, passive versus aggressive, etc. (We'll learn more about these characteristics in Chapter 7, "Labeling your Opponents.") For example, player A is a rock who only bets made hands; player B just sat down, so you don't know him yet; player C is a bluffer who will bet a scary-looking board but fold to a raise; etc.

Yet another thing I like to do is periodically think about how I can apply what I've learned from my opponents in this game to future opponents. I do this by seeing if certain tendencies commonly go together to form a pattern. For example, in hold'em, I've noticed that some low-limit players love to slow-play trips on the flop (generally a mistake). As it turns out, these same players in early position will often bluff that they have the trips if they don't. Now if I see a player who loves to slowplay trips, I'm more likely to raise him if he bets out to represent them—even if I've never played against him before. Most of the time I'll be right and my raise will win the pot; even when I'm not, I'll have learned something about this specific opponent.

6. Never stop watching

Even when you think you've "learned" a player, keep studying him. You may see something new. He may go on tilt, or he may tighten up. He may get tired and loosen way up. He may order a drink. Or he may just keep on playing his regular game, but show you something that you hadn't noticed before. And if he's that rare bird, a good player, you should study him especially hard—you may learn something from him. As Roy West says, "Never stop studying your opponent. Not today. Not next week. Not next year."

7. Watch when you're in a hand, too

Strangely, there are some things you may pick up on better when you're playing a hand then sitting it out. Here's an example of picking up a tell in seven-stud: you made a flush on Fifth Street, and your sole opponent has checked and called on both Fifth and Sixth streets with what appears to be two small pair. He's been keeping his head down the whole way, but now on the river you look up from your own cards to find him alertly looking you in the eye. This should tell you something. In low-limit stud, where relatively few players bluff on the river, the most likely conclusion is that he's made his full house. He's watching you to see if you'll bet for him, allowing him to check raise. (It helps if you've been watching him enough to know if he's astute enough to check raise—some players never do.)

The reason you're more likely to notice this sort of thing when you're *in* the hand, as opposed to being out of it, is that being looked in the eye by an opponent is very personal and immediate; you feel it even more than you see it. However, it takes some experience to be able to pay attention to opponents' behavior when you're playing a hand; most beginners in this instance will be too pleased with their flush to refrain from betting it. They're like happy campers in rattlesnake country, never looking down at the ground as they walk.

8. Once you've discovered your opponent's betting habits, decide on what tactics to use to exploit him.

Once you discover that an opponent plays certain hands predictably or badly, you can exploit this by choosing an appropriate counter-measure. Most counter-measures work best when you're head-up, but they can also work in three-way or four-way action if you have a good read on the other players' likely holdings.

For example, in hold'em, there are habitual slowplayers who always wait till the turn to raise with two pair, trips, or a set, both to disguise their hand and because the turn bet is twice as expensive as the flop bet. Against this sort of player, you'll get more free cards than usual when he checks his big hands; be more prone to check behind him if you think you may be second-best, since he's giving you a free chance to improve and beat him.

Some players never bluff, even head-up. While it's usually correct not to bluff into a multi-way pot, it's a mistake not to occasionally bluff against a decent player when it's just the two of you: never bluffing makes your bets and raises completely predictable. For example, if a player never raises as a bluff or semi-bluff on the turn in hold'em, you can always safely throw your fair hands away when he does raise. Most hold'em players aren't this weak, but you can make a lot of money from the ones that are.

More often you'll run into the sort of player who's overly aggressive: if checked to, he'll always bet, regardless of the strength of his hand. If you're head-up against this type, check your good hands and let him bet them for you; this way he never smells the danger he's in until it's too late. If you were to bet first, on the other hand, he might be more likely to fold. You induce him to bluff by pretending to be weak.

A lengthy list of many different kinds of habits and weaknesses and how to exploit them can be found in Chapter 25 of Sklansky's "Theory of Poker," under the heading "Evaluating the Players and Adjusting to Them." You should read this section, as well as the rest of the book, as soon as you begin to get a feel for this sort of thing and want to know more.

9. *Don't worry in easy games about whether anyone is reading you the way you're trying to read them.*

It should be obvious from all of the above that the best players are the least predictable: they sometimes slowplay and sometimes don't, bluff only as much as required to keep you off-balance, and so on. In loose, easy games such as those commonly found at the low limits, where your opponents' primary mistake is to call with too many hands, trying to play deceptively won't help you and can sometimes hurt you. You're best off playing good cards in a straightforward manner. But as you come up against better opponents, you'll have to begin mixing up your play to avoid them reading you too easily. I won't say any more on that subject, since it's beyond the scope of this book.

10. *Reading techniques can be applied to home games, but it often takes more effort than for casino games*

This may seem to go against common sense. If you play with the same people time after time, you're going to get much better at reading them, right? Well, yes and no. It's true that you'll get better at reading their overall demeanor and picking up on their tells. You'll come to know who's tight, who's loose, and who's just plain wild. But what you won't always be able to do is read their hands as well as you might read the hand of a stranger in a casino.

The reason for this is simple: most home games are dealer's choice. If as many as a half-dozen or more different games are being called with regularity, it's harder to keep track of how players play their hands—a big pair in seven-stud isn't the same thing as a big pair in a wild-card game, and so on. There is simply too much data being tossed about to neatly classify it the way you would playing only one game in a casino.

Even so, attention to your buddies' betting patterns and preferences for starting hands will still pay off. For example, in my own home game, we play a lot of high-low Omaha. There are a couple of players who only feel comfortable betting or raising before the flop with potential nut-low hands like A2xx. If you are holding A2xx yourself, you can fold rather than call and save yourself some money, since at best you are likely to win only a quarter of the pot. Likewise, if you're holding an opposing hand and the flop counterfeits the A2xx, you can play accordingly, knowing the preflop raiser is now crippled.

If you're really fanatic, you can develop your card-reading skills for any given home game—even funky games like Baseball or Chicago. Once you've learned enough about pot odds, implied odds, and advanced concepts such as how loose or tight to play in a given situation, you can develop what you would consider an ideal strategy for a game like Baseball. Then, just as you would for a casino game, you can study your opponents to see if they deviate from the ideal, making mistakes for you exploit. Just don't tell anyone you're doing this if you want to avoid being labeled as an obsessive-compulsive, unsporting fink.

A less time-consuming suggestion for home games is to study your opponents' general tendencies regardless of the game: do they prefer to raise with drawing hands, or only call? Are they canny enough to raise to narrow the field with a marginal hand? Will they only bet and raise with a made hand? What is their degree of poker smarts—do they know what a good hand is for a given game, or are they so ignorant they're going to radiate happiness with a lousy hand and inadvertently make you fold a much better hand?

Now let's move on to classifying common types of low-limit opponents you'll encounter—a poker taxonomy, if you will.

Chapter 7

Labeling Your Opponents

Maniacs, calling stations, weak-tights, rocks: Who *are* these people?

There are a lot of labels used to describe different types of opponents. If you're a poker-book junkie, you're probably familiar with most of these; if not, keep reading. I'll keep things short, but we'll use these labels a fair amount in the chapters to come, and you need to be able to follow along. In addition, players who match up with these labels are commonplace in cardrooms, so you'll get plenty of practice in applying them.

Just bear in mind that while labels are a convenient shorthand, they're no substitute for knowledge of individual habits. For example, in seven-stud, you might discover that the elderly lady you tagged a "calling station" is capable of surprisingly aggressive play—but only on big flush draws, for reasons she keeps to herself. If you're watching her closely, you might stumble onto this; but if you label her once and thereafter get lazy, you'll be surprised.

In addition, key details are often specific to the type of game being played, and thus beyond the reach of a label. An example would be whether an opponent likes to fastplay or slowplay flopped trips in hold'em. We'll talk more about this sort of thing in the chapters to come, on reading hands in hold'em and stud.

The three poker scales

The catch-all labels like "calling station" or "rock" are actually built up from smaller labels—or more accurately, from where a player falls on three different scales of poker behavior. These scales are initially presented as oppositions, like hot versus cold or day versus night, but thinking of them as scales is more useful. Here they are:

- Loose vs. tight

- Passive vs. aggressive

- Naïve vs. knowledgeable

Loose vs. tight

A player can be loose in a number of ways. First, he can play too many starting hands; second, he can call too many raises; third, he can raise with too many hands, exposing himself to reraises from better hands; and fourth, he can go too far with those hands he does choose to play, even if his initial hand selection was tight.

These forms of looseness are all very different. To give an obvious example, if an opponent plays too many starting hands in hold'em, you can take advantage by liberally raising with your good hands after he's limped in—but if you discover that he himself only raises with AA and KK, you do him the honor of folding rather than confuse his loose limps with his tight raises.

A tight player can likewise be tight in these same ways. He can play very few starting hands; call very few raises; raise with very few hands; or fold with relative ease on later streets.

Playing too tight or loose is generally considered a bad thing—but what an expert considers to be too tight or lose will vary, depending on the number of players, how well they play, the betting structure, and other factors. One of the differences between beginners and intermediate players is that the intermediate player does a better job of loosening or tightening up to take advantage of the changing situation. Conversely, a beginner almost never changes how he plays.

Passive vs. aggressive

A passive player hardly ever bets out or raises, and if she does, it's with a very strong hand. An extremely aggressive player, to the contrary, needs hardly any excuse to bet or raise—or even reraise. We'll see later that passivity is one of the hallmarks of a calling station, while mindless aggression is a sure sign of a maniac.

Naïve vs. knowledgeable

We covered this in the proceeding chapter: If your opponent is a poker moron, you must take this into account when considering how much meaning to attribute to his acts; on the other hand, if he's savvy and shrewd, what he does will make a lot of sense, if only you can figure it out in time.

Labels and types

Here they are, in no particular order. Note that most but not all of these are pejorative. There are a few labels here that aren't in common usage, but that I've coined myself to describe player types you may run into; I've indicated these as such.

Rock

As the name implies, a rock seems to sit motionless for hours at a time, waiting for the nuts before playing a hand. You rarely have rocks in a home game—if someone is that tight, they generally aren't invited back. And most home game players like action, not sitting around reading the sports pages or watching the TV while they fold hand after hand. Although tightness is a virtue, rocks are *too* tight—once you recognize them, they're easy to duck when they finally bet their big hand. Meanwhile they're passing up opportunities to steal small pots or play the sorts of drawing hands that win monster pots.

Calling station

In contrast, most home game players exactly fit the description of a calling station: a loose, passive player who plays almost every hand he's dealt, and who will call to the river with a very weak hand on any sort of long-shot draw, or just in case the other fellow is bluffing. Calling stations are death if you persist in bluffing them, but they will pay you off every time you have a good hand. Therefore, you bet for value against the calling station, and never bluff. The worst fate that can befall you at a poker table is to turn into a calling station yourself.

Maniac

Home games have their share of maniacs, too. Often a home game maniac likes to pump it up with drawing hands; on the nights he hits his draws, he wins more than anyone else, but he also has more (and bigger) losing nights than anyone else. Maniacs can shake up a table and get other players to tilt; these players see the maniac playing trash and decide to fight fire with fire, which is usually a mistake.

Maniacs can do quite well if a game is short-handed, because now their lower hand values and high level of aggression are appropriate. In addition, there are smart maniacs and stupid ones—the smart ones are dangerous because although they appear to be constantly jamming the pot, in reality they're selective on later streets, either quietly folding if they don't like how their hand has developed or jamming it some more if they've gotten lucky.

If you can imitate a smart maniac for half an hour, then change gears into a tight, value-oriented mode, you can sometimes devastate players who don't catch on. But this is not something to try against strong opponents, or when you're just starting out.

Tourist

Used disdainfully to indicate players who only visit a casino when traveling. Unfortunately, we're all tourists unless we live in Las Vegas or a similar town. Tourists are further considered to play loosely and badly. Pros think of tourists as walking ATMs, but in most low-limit games you'll see many tourists and very few pros, if any.

Regular or local

The opposite of a tourist—someone who lives near a casino or club and plays there all the time. That doesn't necessarily mean he or she plays well, however. Many regulars are retirees; others are young people who come for the social scene as much as to play.

Young aggressive

This isn't a term in common use, but it's how I think of a particular class of player: young, college-age men who come with their buddies, often buy a lot of chips, and play an aggressive game compared to most of the regulars. Sometimes they're knowledgeable, dangerous opponents who are working their way up the limits; other times they only seem aggressive, but soon reveal flaws in their games and a basically passive nature when they're not dealt the nuts. If you're reading this book, there's half a chance you're a young aggressive yourself.[1]

---

1. There's speculation that at least some of these young aggressives are Matt Damon wannabees, inspired by the movie "Rounders." Who knows? It's certainly a popular film, in spite of the numerous flaws in the poker scenes.

Slumming mid-limit player

Again, not a term in common use, but a type I run into fairly frequently. A player who normally plays $10/$20 or $15/$30 may be waiting around for her usual game and decide to sit down in your comparatively small game to kill time. Watch carefully. A bad slummer will bet too hard against loose-passive opponents with hands like big pairs, lose a few showdowns, and inevitably start bitching that you can't win at the low limits because players don't know enough to fold. A good slummer, on the other hand, knows exactly how to run over your game and may do it just for the fun of it. In the latter case, pay attention and you may pick up a few tricks—though you won't be able to use them until you get as good as the slummer, which won't be for a while.

Drunks

A drunk tends to be either very aggressive or very passive—but in any case, he's almost always very loose. Aggressive drunks can make you a pile of money under the right circumstances, because they insist on pumping money into the pot with totally dominated hands. What's key here is how the rest of the table is handling the situation and if there are any other good players who want to horn in. Drunks can also slow down a game and cause arguments, so they're a mixed blessing.

With our terminology in place, we're now ready to look at the specifics of reading hands and opponents in two popular casino games—hold'em and seven-card stud.

Chapter 8

Reading Hands and Players in Hold'em

L et's make sure you're ready for this chapter. First, you need to have learned at least the rudiments of a sound strategy for low-limit hold'em. Most likely this strategy will be based on a thorough study of the books we discussed earlier, notably Lee Jones's "Winning Low Limit Hold'em." Second, and just as important, you need to have put in some serious practice time against real players, either online at the micro limits, or else at a club or casino.

While studying opponents is a necessary skill, it's a skill that won't do you a bit of good if you haven't accumulated enough playing time. Hold'em is a complex game, even at low limits, and you're certain to make all the classic beginner mistakes before you begin to catch on. Once you do, the added ability to analyze an opponent and his range of probable hands will be a huge bonus, as long as you know how to honor that knowledge by reacting properly. That takes time and experience, and sometimes we stumble along the way.

Here's an example of stumbling that still makes me wince. Playing $3-$6 hold'em at the Mohegan Sun casino in Connecticut, I was congratulating myself on how well I'd categorized one of my opponents, a cowboy type with a mustache. I knew him to be a loose and aggressive re-raiser before the flop, but utterly passive thereafter: he'd always pay you off, but never raise on the turn or river without a very powerful hand indeed. Given his nature, I wasn't surprised that when I raised before the flop with KK he reraised me.

The flop came rags, I bet, Mr. Mustache called; the turn brought a Queen and this time he raised me. I'm sorry to say I paid him off, even though I needn't have: he flipped over pocket Queens on the end, giving him a set—the only hand such a passive player after the flop would have felt confident enough to challenge me with. Given the 22-to-1 odds against my catching one of my two Kings versus the much smaller odds offered by the pot, I should never have called his raise. My categorization of him had been correct, but in the heat of the moment I'd suffered brain-lock. In some ways, poker is like a sport; until you have a move down cold, you can't execute it in real time.

That's my cautionary example—now let's move on.

In section II of "Winning Low Limit Hold'em," Lee Jones gives excellent advice on typical players you'll encounter, similar to our discussion in Chapter 7: loose-passive calling stations, loose-aggressive maniacs, tight-passive rocks, and tight-aggressive solid players such as you should be. He explains how to categorize your opponents by watching how often they limp in, raise, or call a raise. He also suggests analyzing the cards an opponent shows down to help in defining whether you're dealing with a maniac, a loose-passive player, and so forth.

All of this is good stuff—but it's just the beginning. You can and should go much further than that as you begin to acquire experience. To start with, I recommend that you get much more specific in noting how opponents play their cards. Here's an example of what I mean: if you know that a player only raises before the flop with QQ or better and never with any other hand, even something like AKs, then every time she raises you can put her very precisely on any of the three hands she *does* raise with. This may seem too obvious an example to be useful, but I can assure you that such players exist and you will likely be running into them, especially at the low limits.[1] Is

---

1. It's even more common to find players who will only reraise with the biggest of the big pairs, typically KK or AA. More dangerous players will reraise with a wider variety of hands, making them harder to read.

such a player "passive"? Well, that *might* be one way to describe her; but it isn't saying much. The specific knowledge of the hands she will raise with is far more valuable to you in this case.

In this chapter, we'll look at preflop quirks and how to exploit them; a checklist for analyzing opponents; and how reading opponents in short-handed pots is different than in multiway pots. We'll wrap up with a short quiz on reading hands in actual play.

Preflop quirks at the lower limits

As we discussed in Chapter 6, learning how your opponent prefers to play his starting hands is the first step towards reading his hand in future deals. In hold'em, most authorities agree on the proper play of certain hands before the flop, making decent players who adhere to these standards relatively easy to read. For example, if a good but not great player raises under the gun in a full ring game, even if you don't know too much else about him, you can probably still conclude he's got AQ or better for big offsuit cards, AJs or better for big suited cards, and anywhere from 99 on up for pairs. Likewise, if he limps under the gun, the chances are good he's *not* limping with a pure drawing hand if he's a straightforward player and the game isn't particularly loose.

But many low-limit players whom you'll encounter are far less orthodox. It's often said that such players have no standards at all, but simply play "any two cards." This isn't true, however: pay attention and you'll find that some of these players love to limp in with suited trash; others prefer big-little trash; still others will call a raise or even reraise with any pocket pair, no matter how small; and so on. Your reads won't be as precise as they might be against a decent player, but they'll still give you a big advantage. In some cases you'll know absolutely what hand the player has and can call it long before he turns his cards over.

What follows is a sampling of preflop quirks you may encounter at limits such as $2-$4, $3-$6, and $5-$10. Remember, one way to judge your opponent is by how he plays a hand as compared to how you would play it—and this applies especially to starting hands.

Unless otherwise noted, we're assuming a full ring game, with eight to ten players.

Quirk: Never raising with big pairs or big offsuit cards such as AQ or AK before the flop, regardless of position.

Implications: Sometimes it's a good play not to raise with a big pair or big cards, depending on your position and the nature of the game. For example, if six loose players have already limped in, you may want to limp in with AQ on the button rather than raise.[2] Low-limit players who *always* limp in with their big hands, however, are hurting themselves badly. They're failing to earn what they could with monsters like AA or KK, and they're letting opponents see too many cheap flops with drawing hands that can turn AQ or AK into garbage.

At any rate, if such a player springs to life with a bet or raise on the flop, or else raises the turn when a blank hits, just bear in mind that he might have limped in with a pocket overpair or something like AK that has now made him top pair. (Of course, this is in addition to other plausible raising hands, such as two pair or a small set.)

Given his habit of limping, he's probably a passive player by nature, so you shouldn't have any trouble stepping aside if you don't have a very good hand yourself.

---

2. See the chapter on loose games in "Hold'em Poker for Advanced Players" if you don't understand why. This book is discussed in Chapter 13, "Refining Your Game" on page 136.

Quirk: Only raising with very big pairs before the flop; limping with all else.

Implications: If you come across a player like this, you can fold without regret many hands you might otherwise have called or reraised with. For example, with the player I mentioned earlier who only raised with QQ or better, I would have no trouble folding AK or JJ after her raise. If I play AK, for example, I'm buying trouble: two of her three possible hands will destroy me, leaving me only one hand I can beat. And even in that case I'm drawing to beat her.

Quirk: Tough when raising—only raises with big pairs, big off-suit cards, etc.—but loose otherwise, calling too many raises with weak hands.

Implications: If you decide someone is a tough player because of what he raises with before the flop, but ignore the weak hands he will call a raise with, you will be giving him too much respect and wasting opportunities. Likewise, if you characterize him strictly as a loose player because he called your raise when he shouldn't have, you may not respect his raises enough. Don't assume—watch!

Quirk: Raising with sub-par hands before the flop, such as KJs or A9s under the gun, or something like AJ from the blinds with several callers.

Implications: Once you discover a player is a weak raiser, you will sometimes have the chance to isolate them by re-raising—even with hands you'd normally fold. For example, if you would normally fold AJ or 88 to an early raise, you can now reraise if no one else has yet called. This will obviously work better if the player is otherwise passive and will check if the flop doesn't hit him and he isn't holding a big pocket pair. With a more aggressive player, however, you need to be careful and only play on if the flop is to your liking.

In all cases, remember that a weak raiser is raising with a *range* of hands—just because you saw him raise with KJs under the gun doesn't mean he might not have a real hand this time. Also, avoid this play if other players have already called the first raise and will likely call your reraise; after the flop you may find you have the weak raiser beat, only to lose to a third player who stayed in with a legitimate hand.

Quirk: Limping with any two suited cards.

Analysis: Since in low-limit hold'em, most pots are multiway, and since flushes are great multiway hands, why not go for every flush chance you can? The problem is, a hand like 82s has negative expectation: in the long run, the pots you manage to win don't pay for all the times you have to fold after the flop. And keep in mind that even if you make your flush, it will sometimes lose to a bigger flush. So although players who limp in with these sorts of hands will occasionally win a nice pot, in the long run you *like* the fact they're donating their limp-in money to the table.

Keep in mind you will often want to raise or check-raise on the flop to protect hands such as trips, sets, or top pair with good kicker; your goal is to drive out this sort of player if he's hanging around in hopes of a backdoor flush. The same concept applies to players who hang around with three-card straight draws or similar longshots.

Quirk: Playing very tight if no one limps in early, but loosening up and playing too many hands if someone *does* limp in early.

Implications: If an early player limps, this sort of player will jump in with any two suited cards, offsuit cards such as KT that are very weak, and so on. Because of this, you'll sometimes see an entire table alternate between very tight and very loose from one hand to the next, depending on whether the first one or two players limp in or not. If you sense the game has several players of this sort, and if preflop raises are few and far between, try limping when you're under the gun or in second position with drawing hands you normally wouldn't dream of playing so early—J9s, 33, and so on.

If the table is too aggressive and you get raised more than rarely, or if you don't pull in enough limpers, you'll have to desist. And as always, be ready to get off a hand like K5s if you flop something like top pair with a terrible kicker. But otherwise, this is a terrific tactic for exploiting a very loose-passive game.

Quirk: Limping in with drawing hands when playing short-handed (five or fewer players).

Implications: Since drawing hands are long-term money losers in a short-handed game, punish such players by raising them liberally with your good hands like AT, KQ, and so on. Meanwhile, play few if any drawing hands yourself unless you're in the blinds. The best guides to playing short-handed are Jim Brier and Bob Ciaffone's "Middle Limit Holdem Poker," and Sklansky and Malmuth's "Hold'em Poker For Advanced Players," both recommended in Chapter 13.

A checklist for analyzing opponents

It's a good idea when starting out to have a mental checklist of the most important questions to ask yourself about an opponent. After a while the habit of observation will become ingrained and you won't need to be so formal.

Below is my own checklist for this purpose. I put it together when I was teaching myself hold'em, but was pleased to later came across a similar list of questions by poker writer Bob Ciaffone, in his book "Improve Your Poker."[3] My list is more geared to low-limit games than Ciaffone's—but regardless, Ciaffone points out that the quicker you can get a read on an opponent, the better. This is especially true if the cardroom is a busy one and players keep coming and going.

Checklist for evaluating an opponent in hold'em

- *How many hands does he see the flop with? How often does he raise?* I want to get a general read on whether he's tight or loose, passive or aggressive.

- *What will he limp with in early position? In middle position?* I'm looking to see if he plays drawing hands out of position, or conversely likes to limp with raising hands.

- *What will he raise with in early position? In middle position?* I need to know whether to respect his raises—whether he's a solid player who only raises early with big pairs and big cards. If he's raising with weaker hands than he should, then I'll know I can call or even reraise with hands I would normally throw away.

- *What will he reraise with?* Again, I want to know whether to fear his reraises. If he just likes to gamble, that again lets me play a few hands I'd otherwise toss. I still have to exercise discretion, though, because his reraises are increasing the price I'm paying to see the flop and in some cases could trap me in a raising war.

- *What will he call a raise with?* If he has high standards and enters a raised pot, I have to be more conservative about entering that pot myself than I would with a loose player.

- *Does he like to check or otherwise slowplay big hands?* If he always slowplays a big hand, I've got an easy read on him. Conversely, if he is that rare breed who habitually

---

3. The chapter with the questions is called "Sizing Up a Stranger." It's worth reading, as is the rest of the book, even though Ciaffone is talking about middle-limit hold'em most of the time, not low-limit.

fast-plays hands the average player would slowplay—for example, big trips on the flop—I need to know that to protect myself.

- *Is he a passive player who will only bet or raise after the flop with strong hands, or is he aggressive and savvy enough to bet his draws also? Will he bluff-bet the river if he's heads-up but missed his draw, or will he check?* Passive players are better to have in a game because they'll pay off your big hands, while only raising when they have a big hand themselves. With an aggressive player who might be on a draw that missed, you must be more willing to show down your hand on the river so that he doesn't decide you're a weak player he can easily run over.

Reading players when the pot is short-handed

Any time you see the flop either head-up or with only two other opponents, you must change gears: You are now no longer as concerned about calculating the odds as you are about playing the other players. The exact cards you hold matter less, and what takes on importance is your position, the preflop action, and whether your one or two opponents are passive or aggressive, loose or tight, easy to read or tricky.

Here's an example to make things clear: Let's assume it's a full ring game, and that you limped in under the gun with ATs, hoping for a volume pot with additional outs if your fairly weak kicker nonetheless gives you a good Ace. As sometimes happens, the table folds to the big blind, who looks at his cards, shrugs, and checks. It's just the two of you. The flop comes rags, not helping your hand in the slightest; the big blind again checks. What do you do?

First, you should know from your reading that your ATs is a monster compared to two random cards, which is what the blind is holding until proven otherwise. In almost *every case* you would probably bet the flop for this fact alone. But in this case, you have an additional incentive: the big blind is clearly underwhelmed by his hand and *he has checked to you in a short-handed pot.*

Would it matter if you held 73 offsuit which you limped under the gun in a moment of madness? No, it wouldn't. Your cards are immaterial here. You are playing the situation, and your sole opponent has informed you by his behavior that he will gladly fold if you so much as extend a hand towards a chip.

You will often see low-limit players who've gotten head-up check it down to the river. The pot is so small and their cards are so bad they've both given up, and their mannerisms make this clear. Don't ever imitate them. If you do, any good player who happens to be in the game will mark you down as a soft target and start raising more often if it might get them head-up with you. This is certainly what I do against weak, readable opponents.

Here are a few ideas for head-up or three-way action, especially if it wasn't raised preflop or if a late raise might have been no more than an attempt to steal the blinds.[4]

- Against a passive opponent who will call with a hand like bottom or middle pair but never bet it, you are better off checking it down when you hold nothing and have no outs. Doesn't this violate what I just told you, that you shouldn't play soft head-up? Yes—except that you make money from calling stations when they pay you off, not when you pay them off.

- Some tricky players habitually slow-play their good hands head-up. Again, you may be better off playing "weak" those times you don't have a hand by checking after them.

---

4. I'm not including those times that reraises before the flop have limited the action to a couple of participants who likely hold powerful hands. That's a different ball of wax and requires very good reading skills indeed.

This turns their strategy against them, since now they can't make any money when they do hit. Of course, if you actually hold a hand, or even some outs such as a backdoor draw, go ahead and bet.

- Against an average player, you normally should have some value before betting early; this can be bottom pair, an Ace, or a backdoor draw. Of course if you've got position and they've indicated weakness, you should always bet.

- If a scare card comes on the river that logically might have made you a good hand, you should bet if the turn was checked and you're up against a weak-tight player. Most of the time you'll pick up the pot; if you're raised you can fold.

These points don't begin to do justice to the complexities of head-up and three-way play. The best writers on this subject are Bob Ciaffone, in "Improve Your Poker," and Roy Cooke in "The Cooke Collection," although Cooke is relating intelligent war stories rather than giving systematic advice. For more on these writers see Chapter 13.

Quiz on reading hands

Here are a few examples of reading hands in game situations. In each case the read is a simple one, but the resulting action (when properly taken) is effective. All these hands come from actual play. You might try treating this like a real quiz, covering the answer up before thinking about how you would approach the problem.

Situation: It's a home game, dealer's choice. In a previous hand of seven-stud, you observed a player to your left bluff on the river by betting to represent a made straight. His board looked good (he lacked only an inside card), but when called he had nothing, and lost to two big pair. Now the game is hold'em and you're dealing. No one raises before the flop, which comes as three small clubs. This same player is first to act, and after studying the board a moment and then looking around at the other players, he bets. Everyone folds to you. Your hole cards are small, giving you the remote chance of a backdoor straight, but nothing better. What do you do?

Answer: Raise. You already know this player will attempt a bluff with a scary board, and three small clubs on the flop is very scary. Most players with a made flush in his position would be more likely to attempt a check-raise. If he re-raises you here, you can comfortably fold; but as it is, you have put him on the defensive and he will probably check to you on both the turn and the river if he doesn't make a hand. If so, you may want to keep betting to carry through and win the pot. In the actual hand as played, this in fact is what took place.

Situation: An opponent you know to be a tough raiser before the flop, but fairly passive thereafter, raises under the gun. Everyone folds to you; you find you have AA and re-raise, folding the blinds. The flop comes KTT. Your opponent bets. What do you do?

Answer: Raise. You need to find out if your Aces are still good or whether he's got you crippled.

Your logic goes like this: If you've read him correctly as a passive player post-flop, his bet on the flop means either it helped him, or he has a big pair. If he's holding either AK or a big pair such as QQ or lower, he's unlikely to re-raise you here and will likely check on the turn if it's a blank. But if he's holding KK or TT, you're in trouble. He will likely re-raise you right here, or perhaps just wait till the turn when the bet doubles and bet into you again, despite your show of strength on the flop. If this happens, you'll have to fold, since the pot would need to be huge to give you the right odds to chase your two remaining Aces.

On the other hand, if knew your opponent to be loose-aggressive after the flop, you'd be wrong to fold without more information. Same situation + different opponent = different action on your part.

In the actual hand, the player with Aces neglected to do any thinking whatsoever. He smooth-called his opponent's bet on the flop, figuring smugly that with Aces he was still ahead; raised when a blank came on the turn, was shocked by a reraise; and called on the river, only to be shown—what else?—KK.

Situation: You're in the big blind with 22. Two players limp, and then a player you know as a fairly typical preflop raiser makes it two bets. It's an easy call for you, since with the limpers calling behind you you'll be getting 7-to-1 pot odds to try and flop a set, with the hope of additional action if you hit your hand. The flop comes as rags and everyone checks; the turn is also a blank and once more it's checked around. The river is just as dismal and the first two players again check. This time, the preflop raiser shrugs and bets. What do you do?

Answer: Raise! This pot should be yours. Your logic is as follows: since it's been checked around, odds are that no one has made even a pair. The preflop raiser certainly hasn't—his failure to bet either the flop or the turn means he likely raised with two big cards and is now hoping his Ace-high will be enough to take the pot, should anyone be brash enough to call him. You *could* just call, but there's a remote chance one of the other players has paired a card higher than a deuce and will reluctantly call; your raise is intended to squeeze such a player out. You're not worried by whether the preflop raiser will call your raise—though he almost certainly won't.

In the actual hand, the player with the deuces folded and then kicked himself after he thought through the above sequence too late. He had 4-to-1 pot odds just to call; raising would have still given him 2-to-1 pot odds with the probable best hand.

Situation: You hold pocket Tens as dealer. An early player open-raises, the cutoff calls, and so do you, hoping to flop a set. Only the small blind calls behind you. Four players see the flop for two bets each; it comes 665, two-suited in clubs. The early player and cutoff check to you; you bet, hoping that since they called a raise that neither the cutoff nor the small blind hold a Six even in this loose game; besides, your overpair is fragile so you don't want it checked around. The small blind calls, the preflop raiser folds, and the cutoff calls. The turn comes a King, which you don't like to see; the cutoff checks; you bet. Both players call. The river comes a Six, putting trips on board, and to your surprise the cutoff now bets. What do you do?

Answer: Fold. Whenever a loose, passive player bets into you on the end, they've either gotten lucky or were slowplaying. In the actual hand, the cutoff turned a King, but didn't bet it for fear of someone slowplaying trip Sixes. Seeing the third Six fall on the river, he decided it was unlikely anyone was holding the case Six, so he could safely bet his Sixes full of Kings.

Chapter 9

Reading Hands and Players in Stud

B y now you should have a solid strategy for playing low-limit seven-stud. I'm assuming you've read and re-read Roy West, and have at least taken a look at "Seven Card Stud for Advanced Players." I'm also assuming you've gained enough playing experience to get over the hump of playing too loose or playing hands with too many dead cards. The ability to read your opponents' hands won't do you any good if you misplay your own.

Lastly, I'm assuming you know West's lesson on reading hands (Lesson 4) well enough to recite passages in your sleep. Everything I have to say is in addition to his casual but sharp observations.

Boards and game structure

Stud is different than hold'em in that each player has his own exposed cards, commonly called his board.[1] This makes it comparatively easy to read weak players, especially when you put their board together with their playing tendencies.[2] What gets tricky, however, is remembering the exposed cards in hands that were folded on earlier streets. Keep working at this skill; in the long run it will give you a big advantage. There'll be times when you're able to rule out the hand a player is representing, based solely on remembering folded cards.

---

1. Sometimes a writer like West will use "the board" to refer to *all* of the exposed cards around the table. If so, the context usually makes this clear.
2. For an interesting view to the contrary, see Mason Malmuth's essay "Why Hold'em Players Lose at Stud," from his book "Poker Essays III."

Keep in mind that how you react to a read will vary tremendously based on the limit and ante. Low-limit stud isn't just one game—it's several games. First, there's the no-ante $1-$3 or $1-5 game, in which you prefer to play tight and trap opponents into chasing you with weaker hands. Next there's the small over-ante game, for example a $1-$5 game with a $.50 ante, where you must loosen up and chase a bit more yourself, even if you can't steal the antes. Finally there's the prototypical genuine stud game, such as a $5/$10 fixed-limit game with the same $.50 ante as in the $1-$5 game. Here, you focus once again on tight play, but this time with an eye on knocking opponents out. This is how stud was meant to be played.

At the middle and upper limits, the ante gets bigger in relation to the bet size, so correct strategy redoubles the effort to knock opponents out. Players are more likely to represent hands they don't have, raising and sometimes reraising on speculation or scare cards as well as with their good hands. As the deception increases, reading hands gets harder, even as it becomes essential for survival.

At the low limits where you'll be playing, deceptive warfare of this sort is less common. The only players jamming the pot with speculative hands will be loose-aggressive types who do it because they crave excitement, not because they're thinking strategically. Most of your opponents will be easy to read as long as you pay attention.

Player tendencies to look for

Many players always play their strong hands in a particular fashion, rather than vary their approach to match the situation. Here are some common tendencies and what to do about them:

Big pair limpers. Limping with a hand like Aces or Kings is a reasonable strategy in a tight no-ante game, since you'd prefer to do more than just win the bring-in against just one or two opponents with weak boards. *Always* limping, however, is a mistake, since there will be many times you're better off limiting the field to anyone who has already limped in. In any event, you want to keep track of habitual big-pair limpers so you can respond appropriately.

In a no-ante game, if such a player limps in to your right with an Ace as his doorcard, you may be better off not raising with your pair of split Jacks right away. A raise could get you head-up with his possible pair of Aces, whereas if you also limp you not only get a cheap chance to improve, but can fold if he raises on Fourth Street or bet if he checks. (This assumes he tends to bet out with his big pair on Fourth Street rather than go for a check-raise—something else to watch for.)

However, in a game with an ante—say, a typical $5/$10 game—you'd often want to go ahead and raise with your Jacks, either to limit the field and make the Ace pay if he's on a draw, or else provoke him into revealing the true strength of his hand by reraising you or betting out on Fourth Street. Another advantage to this play is that the Ace will have to bet first on Fourth Street unless you make an open pair; this may allow you to bet again if checked to, with the idea of taking a free card if you don't improve on Fifth Street, where the betting limit doubles.

Doorcard-pairing trappers; doorcard-pairing bluffers. You *must* pay close attention anytime a player pairs his doorcard. What you want to learn is if they have a pattern for how they play trips—and how they play scare cards, too. Do they make only a small bet when they trip up? Do they check and just call any bets? Or do they bet the maximum right away? Their actions may vary depending on whether they feel threatened by anyone's board, but you still must look for a pattern.

Much depends on the player's overall style. If a solid player raised on Third Street with a Ten showing and now pairs his

Ten on Fourth Street, look out. On the other hand, if a player who plays one-third of his hands and raises with any high pair flat-called with a Queen on Third Street, and now gets another Queen on Fourth, your response is totally different: if you can beat a pair of Queens, you can call here or even raise if you think it will get you head-up.

It's important to avoid being stubborn about a read, especially when the evidence starts to pile up in another direction. For example, if the bring-in pairs his low doorcard on Fourth Street, it's unlikely he has trips, even if he bets out. But if he reraises or keeps pushing on later streets, you may have to reassess.

Don't make the mistake of automatically raising a player if they've paired their doorcard and bet out. You're thinking that this is a probe on your part, and that if they reraise you can fold your good but not great hand and save money—but many times they'll just flat-call and leave you guessing. You'll have gained no information and may run into a nasty surprise on a more expensive street.

You also want to look out for players who like to represent trips when they don't have them. These same players are often the ones who slowplay real trips. If you *do* get a good read on a bluffer, look for the occasional chance to isolate him with a raise when you think you have him beat.

Players who bet on the come versus those who don't. Aggressive players will predictably bet out or raise with a four-flush; passive players never will. The same applies to straight draws, although it can be harder to put a very loose player on a straight draw given that he may have started with something odious like a one- or two-gap hand. Players who habitually bet on the come are of course more dangerous than those who never do, but even the former will typically check on later streets if they haven't made their hand. Again, see what their pattern is.

Scare-card bettors. A byproduct of the exposed cards in stud is that many players will bet a scary board, regardless of whether it matches their down cards. It's important to assess how likely it is that they have what they are representing. For example, let's say a player who came out betting on Third Street with a King in the door now catches two more suited cards and bets his three-flush on Fifth Street. Do you have a call if you can't beat a flush? The answer is yes, if you have a hand that beats Kings-up or a draw to such a hand. Your opponent's early raise is much more likely to have signified split Kings than a flush draw.

Rocks and other submerged dangers. As discussed in Chapter 7, rocks are passive, relatively tight players who won't bet any hand less than a monster. Because stud has been around longer than some of the other games, it tends to attract an older population—some of whom have developed very predictable styles over many years of playing. In a no-ante game, a typical rock would be a 65-year-old man reading a newspaper and auto-folding. When he puts his sports section down and bets, watch out!

In general, if an opponent only bets out with trips, a made flush, or some other big hand, you have no excuse for ever calling them unless you have a very big hand yourself. What gets tricky with rocks are situations where someone else is driving the betting, you're calling along with a hand you feel may beat the bettor if you make it—but a rock is also calling along. In such cases the rock may have a crushing hand that they aren't betting, whether because they're happy to let someone else take charge or aren't sure what you have.

Quick quiz on hand-reading in stud

Here are just a few problems to give you an idea of stud hand-reading in action. Try treating this like a real quiz, covering the answer up before thinking about how you would approach the problem.

Situation: A $5/$10 game. You complete the bring-in to $5 with a split pair of Queens on Third Street and get only two callers. They both call your Fourth Street bet as well. On Fifth Street you make two pair, but one of your opponents with a Jack for his doorcard catches a second Jack. He is high board, and bets out. What do you do?

Answer: If you've been watching this player, you hopefully have an idea of how he plays trips when he makes them. If the situation hasn't come up yet, though, you'll have to take your best guess. Was his Fourth Street card suited, meaning he could be betting a four-flush with a pair? Is he a semi-maniac, loose enough to call your earlier bets with no more than a low pocket pair? Did you see a Jack (or even two) in hands that have since folded?

If the answer is "none of the above," you're in a bad way. Even if he doesn't have trips, he had to have something to call your bet with a Queen—slowplayed pocket Kings or Aces, for example. And of course it's very possible he called your opening bet with split Jacks and a King or Ace kicker—or a suited Ten or Nine—and has indeed tripped up. With only three players, the pot is on the small side—about $43 after the rake—so this could be a good time to fold. Let's not even get into the fact that if you hit your underpair for a full house, you can still lose to Jacks full!

Situation: At the Bellagio in Las Vegas, you're playing in a loose-passive $1-$5 game with no ante. You make a marginal limp with a pocket pair of Fives and an Eight for your doorcard; to your delight, you trip up on Fourth Street and bet the maximum. A player to your right is hanging in with what appears to be a draw, and to your left a player whom you know to be a rock is also calling along; her only high card is a Queen, which doesn't seem too threatening. Do you keep the heat on with maximum bets and raises as long the rock doesn't catch another Queen?

Answer: You may already be in trouble. Think for a moment about what she thinks *you* have. Your doorcard is small, yet you're betting strongly; therefore she can only conclude that you have either pocket Aces or Kings, or else trips. This means she can beat Aces or Kings—either with Queens up, or more likely with trip Queens (she *is* a rock, after all). Rather than jam the pot, you should check Sixth Street and do no more than call along if either of your opponents bets, hoping to fill there or on the river.

Situation: A $1-$5 game with a fifty-cent ante, a common structure in Atlantic City and the Native American casinos in Connecticut. You discover the dealer has given you split Jacks with an Ace kicker; what could be better? Just then the obnoxious rock to your right, who's been complaining all night about the bad hands he's been getting, throws in the maximum bet with bored assurance—even though his door card is a lowly Four. The two players after him fold, and now the action is to you. You like your Ace overcard; should you raise and get it head-up?

Answer: Only if you enjoy making regular pilgrimages to the casino ATM. Given the steep rake at this limit, even an overante doesn't justify chasing what is very likely buried Aces, Kings, or at worst Queens with your Jacks. Kiss your now-questionable kicker goodbye and fold.

Situation: A $1-$3 no-ante game, the common starter game in both Atlantic City and the Connecticut casinos. You find yourself with split Kings on Third Street. The Queen to your right raises, you reraise, and everyone folds—except a player with a small doorcard, who checked the first time around but now to your surprise puts in the third raise. What do you do?

Answer: Fold. This player is raising into not one but two obvious split pairs higher than his doorcard. He's either got pocket Aces or else trips he slowplayed the first time around. A lot of low-limit players like to slowplay small trips but can be triggered by raises ahead of them into changing their plans.

Situation: Same as above, but this time you are the only obvious big pair with your split Aces. You bet them confidently, but the bring-in—a guy who only just sat down and who you've been told normally plays at a higher limit—raises you in an aggressive manner with his small doorcard. You feel a slumming high-limit player is more likely to try and run over the game; should you challenge him with some aggression of your own?

Answer: Don't let emotions and suppositions rule your decision-making. With so little in the pot, you're better off folding and watching some more hands to find out what this player is really like. In the actual hand, the split Aces called all the way, only to have the seemingly over-aggressive doorcard show down genuine trips with a snort of glee: "Dealt rolled-up!"

Situation: A $5/10 game at a club. The action has been loose and aggressive. The pushiest player at the table, a burly Russian, sat down an hour ago and is already two-thirds of the way through a $300 buy-in. You're the bring-in with a Three as your doorcard—but you hold another Three down, with a King kicker to boot. When the Russian completes to $5 with the Queen of hearts in the door and gets one loose caller, you call too: with $15 in the pot, you're getting 5 to 1 to call the extra $3, and you know from watching him that the Russian doesn't need a pair of Queens to make this bet. On Fourth Street you pair your Three to make trips and bet the maximum $10. The Russian has picked up a second heart and calls; the other player folds, so you're head-up. On Fifth, you don't improve and he catches a third heart. You bet, but he raises. Now what?

Answer: Seriously consider reraising here and betting Sixth Street if you're not reraised in turn. This opponent *could* have started with a three-flush, but given his bet on Third Street, either a pair of Queens or a pocket pair seems more likely. With his aggressive style he'd bet a threatening flush board no matter what he had. If he does have a four-flush here, he could be hoping his raise will induce you to check Sixth, allowing him to take a free card if he doesn't improve. What's more, even if he has the flush, you still have two cards to catch up by making a full house. In the actual hand, the Russian proved to hold only pocket Tens, neither of which was a heart.

Situation: Another $5/10 game—also loose, but less aggressive. You look down to rolled-up Eights after a Queen has raised in front of you, and re-pop it to $10. To your surprise, a grumpy, tightish regular with a King in the door calls the two bets cold, as does the raiser. The Queen is a loose but reasonably competent player; on Fourth Street he picks up an offsuit King while you and the doorcard King both catch non-threatening cards. Both your opponents check and call your bet. On Fifth, the King catches another seemingly innocuous card and bets out. The Queen has added a Ten for a gutshot straight on board, and calls. You are close to certain you have the bettor beaten—but that gutshot straight has you worried. You pick up two red chips to call; then pick up two more. The action comes to you and you hesitate.

Answer: Go ahead, raise it up! You've probably still got the best hand and you've almost surely got the best draw. The Kings could be rolled-up, but one of them is on the other player's board. And even if he hit trips with one of his other cards, they'll be smaller than your trips. The other player is competent, so he's not likely to have raised in early position on Third Street without either split Queens or a high pocket pair. Chances are his straight isn't there yet, and if he happened to start with pocket Tens and now has trips, he'd surely have let you know about it with a raise here.

Situation: A $5/$10 game, but this time on the tight side. An experienced player to your right may have the mistaken impression that you're a weak player who can be stolen from: twice in the last hour he's raised your bring-in when it was folded around to him. Both times his doorcard was higher than anything you held, and you meekly folded. Now it's folded around to him a third time and he again raises, this time with a King in the door. Your upcard is a lowly Three, but underneath you find two live Eights. This is your chance to call his bluff, right?

Answer: Don't *call* his bluff—raise it! Sure, he could have split Kings or a pocket pair. But it's more likely he doesn't, since he's raised three out of three times in this situation. What's more, your pair is hidden, so you can make trips without him knowing. Be prepared to bet Fourth Street if checked to and take a free card on Fifth if you don't improve. Often, you'll win the pot right here with this reraise, and that's fine too. Situations of this type come up often in games with an ante. In a game with no ante, of course, you'd be well advised to fold your Eights to a raise from a King, with only the bring-in plus the King's raise for equity.

Chapter 10

Reading Players with Tells

"**I** can do that all day," the con man Mike says to the uptight woman psychologist in the opening of the movie "House of Games," having twice in a row guessed the hand in which she is hiding a coin. "How? You got a tell. It's your nose. You're pointing to the coin with your nose."

A wonderful movie, "House of Games"—but tells are seldom as simple as Mike the con man makes them seem, especially when it comes to poker.[1] They're definitely not the first thing you should be thinking about when you're trying to read your low-limit opponents. Betting habits and hand preferences are far more important, as we've seen in the preceding chapters.

Tells *are* useful—but only when combined with other information you've picked up about your opponent. They're rarely useful by themselves, a point neglected by many poker books. Even Mike Caro's otherwise excellent "Book of Tells" is too simplistic in this regard. According to Caro, a player either loves or hates his hand, is either bluffing or not bluffing, and that's all you need to know. But Caro was writing primarily about draw poker—an outdated, relatively mechanical game with only two rounds of betting, and with some structural peculiarities that by all reports encouraged grotesquely obvious tells.[2]

---

1. It's worth noting that the poker game in the opening of "House of Games" is also unrealistic. Is there anyone left alive who still plays five-card draw for big stakes these days?

2. Mason Malmuth, in "Poker Essays, Vol. II," writes that tells were such a large part of draw poker that when he switched to playing hold'em, "it seemed like someone had suddenly 'turned the sound off.'"

The games popular today have more rounds of betting than draw and allow for more complex strategies; as a result, tells occur less often and require more context. You should still read "Book of Tells"—recently re-released as "Caro's Book of Poker Tells"—but more for its ideas than for advice about specific giveaways. For example, Caro draws the important distinction between players who are unconscious of their behavior ("non-actors") and those who are trying to mislead ("actors"). His famous maxim for the latter category is, "Strong means weak, weak means strong." In other words, someone who splashes the pot with bravado probably has a weak hand, while someone who bets with a sigh probably has a powerhouse.

That said, let's go into what I know about tells.

Generic tells vs. individual tells

In writing his opus, Caro focused on tells exhibited by different players in the same situation—generic tells, in other words. There are some useful generic tells in games like hold'em and stud, and I'll mention these shortly. But I have actually found it more worthwhile to study players for their *individual* mannerisms. In the game that starts off Chapter 6, this was how I picked up that my opponent smiled whenever he caught a helping card. It wasn't a big smile, but it was big enough to give him away. In that same game, coincidentally, I also picked up on a buddy's tell: whenever he liked his first three cards in stud enough that he intended to bet or raise when the action got to him, he'd rest his chin on his hand as if bored. I kept telling him ahead of time when he liked his hand, until finally I gave in and told him how.

Even top players have tells; in "Super/System," Doyle Brunson relates that Amarillo Slim picked up a tell of Brunson's in which Brunson would count his chips before betting when he had a real hand, but just push them in without counting when he was bluffing. Some pros feign tells to keep opponents guessing, but at the low limits you're not going to have to worry about this degree of trickery. There's just not enough money at stake.

The one sort of generic tell that I *do* look for is when an opponent betrays emotion or excitement. A player who starts jiggling his foot or tapping his fingers, for example, may have just picked up a great hand; pay attention to see if this is a consistent behavior. Brunson writes that the most reliable sign of excitement is the pulse at the base of the neck, but I've never found that one useful; then again, I'm not a former world champion, either. You're more likely to notice that the player next to you just sat up straight after looking at his hole cards, or that his shoulders slumped for a moment after he peeked at his river card. Recreational players with powerful hands often radiate confidence, but this can be difficult to see if you're involved in the hand and wrestling with your own emotions.

Telegraphs

The kind of tell my buddy exhibited—trying to pretend boredom when he loved his first three cards in stud—is also called a *telegraph* by some writers. This is because it telegraphs your intentions early on. You don't care about telegraphs to your right, obviously—only to your left, from the players who will act after you. Players in both hold'em and stud are capable of telegraphing, but I've found that the way in which they do so differs between the two games.

Telegraphs in stud

Chip-grabbers. Aggressive players in low-limit stud often display a classic Mike Caro tell: if they like their hand on Third Street, they'll grab or fondle some chips from their stack.[3] They're so eager to bet or raise with their good cards that they unconsciously leak information to anyone watching. It's such a common tell that I always look for it as a way of saving money. Here's an example: If I'm thinking of limping in with a hand like a small three-flush, but the Ace doorcard three seats to my left has just grabbed some chips, I can safely fold my drawing hand and avoid getting sucked into a raised pot.

Premature folders. Many tight low-limit stud players develop a characteristic way of folding, and will give themselves away in advance—for example, by holding their downcards in such a way they can use them to flip their doorcard over when the time comes. So if you know that the King and Jack behind you both hate their hands, you can go ahead and raise with a pair of Sixes and steal the antes.

Telegraphs in hold'em

I haven't seen much chip-grabbing in hold'em. Probably this is because hold'em is much more of a positional game than stud, and more players have trained themselves to wait until the action gets to them to look at their hands. Even so, there are still a couple of telegraphs to watch for:

Premature folders. They're nearly as common in hold'em as in stud, especially when players relax their discipline during a long sit. Usually the telegrapher will hold his two cards loosely in his fingers, ready to flick them into the muck. As in stud, this can widen your raising opportunities with fair hands. In a passive game, it can also alert you to throw away a drawing hand early if the players behind you seem ready to fold.

Big-hand statues. Sometimes a player who has snuck a look at his hand and discovered it's raising material will keep stiller than usual until the action gets to him. He may even move his

---

3. Caro mentions that some players don't actually grab their chips, but merely glance at them and then look away; I've seen this behavior less often and it's harder to catch.

hands away from his chips, almost the opposite of the chip-grabber. This is because he doesn't want to scare off any limpers before he raises with his Aces or Kings. I see this more often in hold'em than in stud, but it's usually subtle when it occurs.

Tells on later streets

Once a hand progresses, tells generally fall into the more general category of a player either catching a good card and radiating happiness or confidence, or missing a draw and sagging in some way.

A player who bets mechanically is often so confident of winning that for him the suspense is over. Hence he seems bored. (This is also a great tell for home games, by the way, where mortal locks are common because of wild cards or nut low hands.)

The only trick here is that in deciding what a tell is worth, you must also assess the player's degree of poker knowledge and his range of possible hands. Watch out for weak players who overvalue second-best hands—just as when they bet or raise with a weak hand, they'll have you throwing away the winner because you took their tell too seriously. This is particularly true in hold'em, where weak players can get overly excited about two pair versus a straight board, or a straight versus a flush board.

Caro's "weak means strong" maxim is important to remember when you get to the river in stud versus a weak player with a scary board; low-limit players will often smack down their chips with authority when they didn't make their hand and would rather you fold. The pot odds generally dictate a call anyway in such a situation, but an acting job makes it imperative. In fact, if your own hand is better than your board would indicate, you could consider raising here; if he's bluffing he may fold, and you may have him beaten even if he calls.

In games where bluffing can be a high-percentage play, such as in pot-limit or no-limit, it's probably worth watching for tells related to this—but in limit poker I haven't found this to be the case.

Avoiding tells yourself

The best way I know of to work on avoiding tells and telegraphs is to play at the same table with a friend, so each can watch the other for giveaways. After the game, share anything you picked up. In addition, I try not to look at my starting hands in both stud and hold'em until the action gets to me; that takes care of telegraphs.

That's what I know about tells; happy hunting!

SECTION 3

Getting Better

Chapter 11

Avoiding Strategic Mistakes

To win at poker, it's not enough to know theory and technique, or to be capable of playing an occasional hand brilliantly. You can know every semi-bluff in every book from Sklansky to Ciaffone, you can have the odds tables memorized, and you can calculate odds with the speed of a Pentium IV computer chip—and you can *still* be a long-term loser.

Why? Because in poker, consistency is everything. Since the randomness of the cards bounces our results up and down, and since we must play for hundreds of hours and fold many thousands of hands before getting any idea of how we're doing, we must play *every* hand we can as well as we can, starting with the easy ones. By "easy," I mean hands where what you should do is reasonably obvious—for example, folding a straight draw in hold'em when the pot is small and there's a ton of action on a paired flop. A tricky situation, by contrast, might be where you've played back with a small pair against a possible ante-steal in seven-stud by an aggressive but smart opponent. He might try anything on Fourth Street, but you've got a lot of room for creativity too.

There are more obvious situations in poker then tricky ones, so if you play three tricky situations with inspired genius but muff four out of 10 obvious situations, you'll likely wind up a loser. On the other hand, if you play only one of the tricky situations well but ace all 10 of the obvious situations, you've got a good start towards being a long-term winner.

Other factors matter too, such as game selection. If you're eating up a low-limit game with loose-passive players and then jump to a bigger game with loose-aggressive players, you'll probably lose at first just because you haven't adjusted to the difference in playing styles; even if you play well from the start, your variance will be greater because aggressive opponents are harder to read. In addition, if you're intimidated by the larger bet size, you're now enough of a dog that you should practice wagging your tail in front of the mirror.

Now make it even tougher on yourself. If your new big game has some structural differences you don't understand—for example, anyone who wins two pots in a row must post a kill blind equal to twice the big blind, and the limit likewise doubles for the duration of that hand—you're pretty much *guaranteed* to experience a sudden sharp downturn in expectation that will have you playing at a fifty-cent limit for the next few months while you replenish your bankroll. Getting in over your head in poker is like a car accident: you know it while it's happening, but it's a blur that won't slow down and let you get back in control. Only after it's over do you have a chance of reconstructing what happened.

At one time or another everyone has stumbled or bumbled, even the top poker authorities who tell the rest of us how to play.[1] It's part of learning to handle poker *away* from the table, as an ordinary person who occasionally screws up in other ways, such as overeating or not working out enough.

So this chapter and the next are all about getting more consistent—in other words, avoiding the most obvious kinds of mistakes. In this chapter we'll talk about strategic mistakes, by which I mean mistakes that are technical or managerial in nature; in the next chapter we'll cover emotional and physical mistakes, such as playing when you're angry or tired.

---

1. The exception is David Sklansky. I've never read anything of Sklansky's where he confesses to jumping to a game that was too big for him, or to any similar mistake—but Sklansky never seems quite human anyhow.

Strategy mistakes are your friend—when other people make them

Mistakes are the number one reason you win at the low limits as a recreational player. You're not Doyle Brunson, but you don't have to be: most of your opponents will be bad players who don't know proper strategy and are constantly making one wincing goof after another. That's why winning at the medium and higher limits is harder—fewer of your opponents at those limits will so cheerfully throw themselves on their own sword.

The most common technical mistake, and the one that makes you the most money, is when your opponents play too loose. They play too many starting hands, call too many raises, and go too far with the hands they do play.

The second most common mistake bad players make is to play too passively, betting or raising only with very powerful hands. By ducking the way you'd duck a telegraphed punch, you can starve these players of the chips they'd earn if they were more aggressive, more deceptive, or both.

What bad players are really doing with their loose calls, and their loose calls of each others' raises, is constantly shuffling the same chips back and forth, the total pool shrinking as the house takes its cut. Meanwhile, you stay aloof until you catch a hand that offers positive expectation.

At least that's how it should go in theory. In practice, it's all too easy to make simple mistakes in technique, game selection, and so on, with the result that you throw away your edge. We're not talking here about emotion or fatigue—just miscalculation and misjudgment.

What follows is an incomplete list of such trips and traps. The list is incomplete because everybody has different strengths and weaknesses; yet most of these will cost you chips sooner or later, as they have me and players I know. Fortunately, none of them are fatal and most are quite curable.

Not playing tight enough

This can bite you at any point: Not only when you're first learning a game, as described under the heading of "Playing tight: how tight is tight enough?" in Chapter 4, but later on, when you've begun outplaying many of your less-informed opponents. At this stage you'll be tempted to play more starting hands and go farther with marginal holdings on later streets—but if you take it too far you'll become just another chip-shuffler, albeit with fancier moves.

The solution from a technical point of view is to keep checking up on yourself, for as long as you continue to play poker. Every time you have a losing session, look at your starting hand choices: Were they too loose? Were they appropriate to the situation? Do the same with your play on later streets: Were your calls justified by the odds, or did you get sloppy or fancy?

You should always have a basic, fairly tight starting hand selection to fall back on whenever needed, and a similar basic strategy to fall back on for the later streets. If you're unsure of your decisions, tightening up may cost you some earning power, but it will do a better job of keeping you afloat until you regain touch and confidence.

Often, there's an emotional component to playing too loose. We'll address this more fully in the next chapter, but tightening up technically never hurts as a beginning.

Folding when you shouldn't

This is the opposite disease and less likely to strike; however when it *does* strike, it can be devastating, since it typically costs you not just a single bet but an entire pot. To be precise,

I'm talking about folding on the river because you read an opponent as having the winner and yourself as second-best.

Decent players, and even some bad players, will bluff on the river head-up with a scary board, representing a flush, a full house, etc. But they may have missed their draw or failed to fill; and in any event, you don't want them to start thinking they can run you over by bluffing in the future. So most of the time at the low limits you should call in such situations, as long as you have a half-way decent hand yourself. Tightening up in such situations is a major mistake.

Once you get good at reading opponents, of course, you'll be able to save yourself many bets here: you'll know who bluffs a missed draw and who checks, who's passive versus tricky and aggressive, etc. But until your reading skills develop to this degree, do yourself a favor and call.

In some cases you're right to call even against *two* opponents who both feature scary boards, depending on their skill level and their degree of poker knowledge. One might be bluffing and the other one calling with a weak hand "to keep him honest." If you have a strong but possibly second-best hand—for example, big trips in stud versus two possible flushes—you will hold the winner often enough to justify calling a single bet, though probably not a raise.[2]

Calling more than raising or folding

Winning poker almost always calls for aggression. This can mean reraising or folding rather than calling a raise preflop or

---

2. The pros analyze situations like this as they would any other set of odds—that is, by applying mathematical expectation: What's the cost of calling, versus the size of the pot multiplied by the percentage of times I'll win? If the bet to me is $4 with no chance of getting raised, the pot is $40, and I think I'll win 10 percent of the time, I'm breaking even over the long run. If the bet is smaller or the pot bigger, I'm winning.

on Third Street, open-raising rather than limping in, raising on a later street to knock an opponent out and give yourself a better shot at winning a pot, etc.

If you notice yourself calling more than normal, you may have fallen into a passive poker trance, forgetting to be aggressive. It's easy to do, especially if you're sitting at a table with other passive players; such an attitude can be infectious. One example is agreeing to chop the blinds if everyone folds to you: It may keep the game sociable, but it reinforces passivity. If this sort of thing is a problem for you, you may want to decline chopping as a way of keeping yourself sharp.

Other reasons for slumping into passivity are playing a lot of weak drawing hands in a row, or folding bad cards for hours; both tend to take you out of the game, and when you're out of the game you can get listless and cease to pay attention. A good idea is to take frequent breaks, getting up and walking around the casino for several minutes or even longer—as long as necessary to snap you out of your trance. You may not get better cards when you sit down, but you should be more alert and ready to attack if you do catch a hand.

Even bad air can lull you into a trance: I've noticed that when I play at a particular casino I won't name, the air is stuffy and I have a harder time staying sharp, whereas at another casino with a smaller poker room, the room is better ventilated and I feel more alert and play a little better. Again, a brisk walk will help, as will deep breathing exercises if you don't want to get up from the table immediately.[3]

---

3. I'm not kidding. You need oxygen to think, and deep breathing helps better than junk food, soft drinks, or caffeine. The breathing exercise I find most helpful for this purpose is called "bellows breathing," and is described by Dr. Andrew Weil on p. 205 of the paperback edition of his book "Spontaneous Healing."

Not remembering to stay focused on your opponents

Like getting passive, this is a danger that often strikes when you've been folding hands too long. It's easy to get bored and stop caring about the opposition, especially if you feel you've got a good read on them and none of them is a threat. The problem is that when you're finally dealt a hand you want to play, you won't be alert. You may get one player's habits confused with another's, or you may not notice that a new player sat down, or you may simply mishandle the situation—all because you let your alertness slip away.

Again, the cure is generally to get up and take a break the moment you feel yourself slipping. When you come back, focus on your opponents as if you never saw them before. You can also try some of the tricks mentioned in Chapter 6, most notably stepping away to write down what you do and don't know about each player sitting around the table.

Jumping into a hand when you've just come back to the table

All this stepping away from the table to refresh yourself raises another danger: If you sit back down and immediately catch a playable hand, you may not have fully re-focused. Or a new player may have sat down in your absence, and now he's raised you and you're not sure how to read his raise. In my case, I'm prone to overplaying hands and blowing off chips where normally I wouldn't.

If you find this to be a problem, the cure is to play a little more conservatively when you first sit back down. Take an extra few seconds to decide each action, and be careful of players who are new to you.

Failing to exercise good game selection

Before you make any commitment to play in a given game, consider whether you have an edge or not. This can be when you get to the casino and evaluate the cardroom scene—table A has a lot of laughing gamblers splashing their chips around, while table B features three or four grim sharks you recognize from a higher limit. Which table do *you* want to play at? Or it can be when you're planning a road trip with a buddy—he wants to go to Casino X where the action is supposed to be hot, but as it happens, that casino doesn't spread a low enough limit for you to feel comfortable.[4]

If you can't identify your exact edge over a game, or if some aspect makes you uncomfortable, you're better off not playing. Losing is never fun; nor is burning off your bankroll only to later realize your mistake.

If you're doing well at your current limit, of course, it's correct and natural to experiment from time to time with a bigger limit or tougher opposition—how else can you develop your skills and move up? But be selective and try to stay in control. Your best shot is if you exercise your judgement *before* sitting down to play. It's much easier not to play in the first place then to walk away from a game once you've gotten stuck. More on this in Chapter 12.

Here are some specific questions that may help in game selection:

- Is it a form of poker you're currently practicing? If you don't play much high-only Omaha, for example, you may get your clock cleaned by players who know hand values where you're forced to guess.

---

4. If your buddy is insistent, try to get him to stake you a percentage of the higher limit. I've done this and it can satisfy both players if you're adult about the possibility of losing.

- Are you better than most of the players, or are most of them better than you?

- Is there any one player you fear? If so, try to choose a seat where you'll minimize his impact.[5]

- Is the game passive or aggressive? An aggressive game is more fun but harder to beat, with more variance.

- What's the mix of bluffers versus readable, weak players? Even bad bluffers aren't as profitable as truly weak players. You can still make money from bad bluffers, however, by inducing them to bluff as much as possible.

- If you're playing online at home, is there anything that might distract or irritate you, such as children who need attention, your spouse or partner, etc.? If so, you're better off waiting until you can play without hassle or guilt. Is the limit acceptable for your bankroll? If you're experimenting with a higher limit, set yourself a maximum session loss and stick to it—if you feel it necessary, leave your ATM card and any extra cash at home.

---

5. If you spot a strong, aggressive player but the game is otherwise soft, here's my suggestion: try to sit about three seats to his left. If you sit *immediately* to his left, he'll be raising your blind or ante all night long; if you sit too close to him on his right, you'll have to tighten up on your starting hands for lack of information. Three seats to his left gets you out of reach of his steal-raises and lets you duck his legitimate raises.

Chapter 12

Avoiding Physical and Emotional Mistakes

Although we play poker sitting down for long stretches of time, it's misleading to think of it as game involving only the mind. It's really a body-mind sport. Consider Garry Kasparov, the brilliant chess champion: he's constantly working on new openings and new gambits, but his most important daily training takes place *away* from the chessboard. He's a fitness fanatic, a middle-aged man keeping himself in shape so he can compete against men in their 20s who would otherwise have a huge mental and physical advantage against him. If you want to play consistently good poker, why should you be any different than Kasparov?

In this chapter we'll cover physical mistakes and emotional mistakes. The most common physical mistake is playing when you're too tired to know better; the most common emotional mistake is known as tilt, and consists of letting anger or other negative emotions influence your decision-making. I hope to convince you that these kinds of mistakes are the worst you can possibly make, and are far more damaging than technical glitches like playing too many starting hands or miscalculating the odds.

Picture a bicycle tire that needs to get pumped up every few days because of a tiny puncture. That's what purely technical mistakes are like—you leak chips, but slowly, sometimes so slowly you don't even notice if you're having a good run of cards. Now picture a blow-out of that same tire. In the space of just a few hours, you lose 30 or 40 big bets *or more*—all because you insisted on playing when you weren't at your best. That's the level of danger we're talking about.

Technical mistakes are still the ultimate cause of all losses—physical and emotional mistakes simply lead you to commit more technical errors than usual. But for most players, technical knowledge and self-management are different issues and must be dealt with as such. Going back to the analogy with Kasparov, his technical knowledge of chess is immense—but even the mighty Kasparov has been observed to get rattled or physically exhausted and lose a match in part because of this. Poker players are no different, even the best.[1]

How to handle fatigue

Not everyone loses their sharpness as easily when they're tired. Some players fall apart quickly the moment fatigue sets in—I'm one of these. Others claim they can keep going with only a slight loss in edge, although this assumes your edge is bigger than is feasible for most recreational players. Among top player-writers, David Sklansky has written that he'll stay in a game as long as humanly possible, if he thinks he's still a favorite; Bob Ciaffone, on the other hand, confesses to playing poorly when tired, meaning he has to skip some of those juicy all-night games to avoid becoming a fish himself. You'll have to be the judge in your own case, but it's a pretty fair guess that your model shouldn't be Sklansky.

Let's assume you've discovered through trial and error that you don't play well beyond a certain degree of tiredness. The problem now becomes how to exercise good judgment if you're tired enough that your judgment has slipped a little too. All too often, the lure of the cardroom overcomes common sense. You drove or flew a long way to get to this casino, and even

---

1. Doyle Brunson, Stewart Reuben, and Roy Cooke are among the top players who have written strong cautions about the need for self-management. Brunson's own standards in this regard, however, were superhuman—when he wrote "Super/System," he considered himself capable of playing at his best for 36 hours straight.

though you're jet-lagged or otherwise fuzzy, the heck with that—you can't wait to get out on the floor and *play*.

So how do you make a good decision under such circumstances? One way is to test yourself with a prearranged quiz if you have any doubt of being sharp. John Fox, author of the notorious out-of-print draw-poker classic "Quit Work, Play Poker, and Sleep Till Noon," also advises "a little mental test" for use before playing, such as trying to multiply numbers in your head. In Fox's case, he was a bridge player as well, and used to keep old newspaper columns on bridge handy to make sure he was capable of working out a tough bridge problem or two before playing that game.

Below are four quick questions I use for this purpose. I won't pretend they always do the job—I'm human too, and if I've driven half a day to get to a casino, I'm as prone as anyone to reach for the coffee. But overall they help me save money by detecting those times I'm clearly unready to play.

Quiz: Are you sharp or tired?

Ask these questions of yourself *before* you step into the cardroom. If you display any symptoms, think about taking a nap, going for a walk, or otherwise tuning up instead of playing.

- Unfocused stare or zoned-out feeling while a passenger in a car, waiting in line, watching TV, etc.

- Poor balance. (Balance is a key neuromuscular indicator. Try standing on one foot with your eyes closed to check yourself out—if you start to topple immediately, you're zonked.)

- Forgetful or absent-minded. (Can't find your car keys, lose track of the conversation, etc.)

- Can't do simple math in your head. (Try writing down a few easy problems when you're sharp, then doing them when you know you're tired. See the difference?)

How to handle cardroom seduction

Here we come to the sort of emotional mistake that's relatively subtle, but can still hurt your poker. I mentioned above that just walking into the cardroom can strongly influence you towards playing even when you shouldn't. Taking it a step further, this overwhelming urge to play also applies to sitting at the table too long: you can easily get into a state of mind where you're loath to get up just to take a bathroom break, let alone take a walk or go to dinner. The quality of your play can be going to pieces, but you don't see it; you insist to yourself that you're playing reasonably well, sure you made a few mistakes, but you can tighten up, you're not really tired ... take a break? No way. You've got to sit there till you catch a good hand!

I find it helpful to remember that going to a casino shouldn't mean just sitting at the card table for every possible second of every possible minute. That's seldom fun, even if you're winning—and you're more likely to win if you relax and try to have a complete experience. If the casino has decent restaurants, go have an actual, sit-down meal in peace. Walk around and look at the people. Maybe there's a side-show to take in, such as the chess and pool championships sometimes featured at the casinos near me in Connecticut. If there's an outside to look at—say you still haven't gotten enough of the Strip in Vegas—go outside for a bit. There game will *always* be there when you come back. (Don't be absent from your table for more than two dealer shifts, though, or they may bag your chips—see Chapter 2, "Key Differences between Casino Poker and Home Poker.")

How to recognize and cope with tilt

Tilt can be nearly invisible, even to the player involved, or it can be as obvious as an elephant sitting on the table. If you're feeling stuck and this feeling has persuaded you to start calling too much on the river, an observer who doesn't know you might not realize this isn't your usual playing style. On the other hand, if you're cursing out opponents and throwing cards at the dealer, it's obvious to the entire cardroom that you're unlikely to be playing your best poker just now.

Whether tilt is obvious or not often depends on what's causing it. Let's examine two of the most common causes—poor starting cards, a situation which typically leads to mild tilting, and bad beats, which typically lead to tectonic events on the scale of Mount St. Helens.

Bad starting cards

You haven't you played a hand for the last two hours—or is it three? At any rate, you're desperate to get into a pot, and certain starting hands are therefore starting to look good to you. In fact you can almost hear them whispering to you. That split small pair in stud, for example, even though a Queen just raised the bring-in: maybe the raiser doesn't really *have* Queens. Or that J6s under the gun in hold'em: maybe if you limp in with this dog and nobody raises behind you, you'll flop a nice flush draw. What's the harm?

The harm is that if you let variance distort your judgment (and a long run of worthless starting hands is nothing more than variance), you'll start leaking chips faster then before. It's like deliberately boring a hole in the bottom of a leaky canoe. Instead of patiently bailing, you're trying to sink faster!

Bad beats

It's a truism that several bad beats in a row can unnerve even a good player, turning him into either a calling station or a maniac. You think you're playing smart, but an aggressive player fools you into folding the winning hand; you think your full house is guaranteed, but the worst player at the table shows you quads which he merely called with; and so on. Before you know it, you're playing with all the cool, reasoned skill of Mr. Hyde.

Nine ways to beat tilt

Tilt is so powerful that it's easy to feel helpless—that's provided you've wised up enough to realize you *are* tilting. But recognition is the hardest step; after that, counter-strategies are available to help you drive the beast back into its den and keep it there most of the time. The list below summarizes nine of these counter-strategies; I suggest you try them out whenever you feel tilt is a problem. You should find yourself getting upset less often and less seriously, and enjoying poker more.

1. Don't be in a hurry. Don't expect to win a certain percentage of sessions. Variance being what it is, you can lose many sessions in a row, or vice versa. None of this has much meaning. The number of chips at your seat is only good for playing hands with, not counting as winnings.

2. From time to time, do some additional reading and exercises to get a better feel for variance when you're not emotionally involved. Let's say you have a problem playing as tight up front in hold'em as you know you should: A simple but effective exercise is to deal out 26 hold'em starting hands in a row from a deck of cards, imagining in each case that you're under the gun. Which hands would you play in a tough game? In a passive game? Which would you automatically throw away? You may be surprised at the result.

3. While actually playing, don't focus on winning as your goal. Instead, focus on playing each hand well. Congratulate yourself for good plays, not for stacking chips.

4. Keep score by the month, the quarter, or the year, not by each session; a session is simply too small a snapshot to give you an accurate picture of how you're doing.

5. Work on your skills to try and weed out bad habits and mistakes, but don't beat yourself up when you lose; remember that even very good players have losing months.

6. Stay mindful of your emotions at the table. You can consciously pause before a decision and feel whether you're excited, angry, resentful, frustrated, etc.; you can then examine your impulse to make a given play and see if the emotion is driving it. Think about what the correct play is, as opposed to the impulsive play. This is a very powerful tool for the emotional player, as many of us secretly are.

7. Don't get wild versus wild players, tricky versus tricky players, or over-aggressive with aggressive players. In other words, don't try to fight fire with fire. Remember that the better class of wild or loose-aggressive player is *trying* to get you to tilt by chasing him; that's how he makes his money. Frustrate such a player by playing a solid game with strong cards. You may need to call more often with your fair hands, and you can try on occasion to isolate a loose raiser—but do so as part of a plan, not because you want to get even.

8. Quit if you've lost your buy-in. This may seem like a cop-out, but it will keep tilt away. It avoids other problems, too: many poker writers agree that you're more of a target when you're losing, since other players are no longer intimidated by you and indeed may feel they have a better chance of bluffing you or running you over with raises.

9. Quit before you go numb to losing. Mike Caro writes of exceeding the "threshold of misery"—meaning that if you

lose more than a certain amount, you no longer care what else you lose in the deluded quest to get even. Quit *before* you get to this threshold, not after.

Don't let tilt make you rude

I don't want to let this subject go without reminding you that tilt calls for your best behavior, regardless of whether it's you tilting or an opponent.

If you're the one tilting, do your best to avoid letting it push you into shouting, card-throwing, nasty remarks, or other displays of rudeness. It's not the dealer's fault you've gotten terrible starting cards, nor your opponents' fault that you're losing. Even if an opponent calls your powerful raise with some weak trash hand when he shouldn't, then draws out on you with a miracle card, it's *still* not his fault. You actually want him to play this way, because in the long run, his bad play makes you money. Don't complain, whine, or lecture him on his mistakes; instead, congratulate him on his masterful play so he'll be encouraged to make further loose calls.

I've noticed that some players taunt opponents who are on tilt, in hopes of tilting them still more. This is a bad idea. First, it goes against the general rule that you want relaxed, cheerful opponents, since they're more likely to gamble; and second, an opponent you've goaded may decide to tighten up and play better as his best chance of getting back at you. Lastly, I don't know about you, but I play poker to enjoy myself—not to contribute to bad feelings in the world.

Poker is a strange game in this respect: By mutual agreement we attempt to prey on each others' weaknesses—and yet the most successful players typically work hard at making their opponents feel comfortable and appreciated, not despised and abused.

The ultimate enemies: addiction and obsession

Poker is a game of occasional, random reinforcement: bad hands predominate, good hands are few, we often lose and feel crummy about it—yet when we finally win a hand or a session, we feel terrific and forget how lousy we felt just a moment ago. Scientists who have studied environmental influences on human behavior describe this sort of situation as having a high potential for addiction: we're like the laboratory rat feverishly pressing a lever to get that elusive, occasional dose of cocaine. The rat may die of starvation before it is willing to quit pressing the lever; as humans, we have slightly more control over our behavior, but perhaps not as much as we like to think.

In addition to addiction, poker also lends itself to obsession, since it is multi-layered enough that we can easily get lost in it as a pure intellectual challenge. Like any other obsession, poker is intensely time-consuming: we have to fold an enormous number of hands just to get a chance to exercise our skills. Hours and days can evaporate as we sit waiting for these good hands, with the net result that we may seem upon recollection not to have been much alive during that time. The only evidence of something happening is a gain or loss in our bankroll. If the change is slight, as is often the case, we may be driven to conclude that we played all day to win or lose that small sum, say four dollars.

If you think I'm exaggerating the danger of poker as a hobby, I invite you to read "Poker Faces," a sociological study of the draw poker scene in Gardena, California, in the 1970s. This text by writer David Hayano is a bit dry at times, but it gives you a picture not only of the professional players who were Hayano's ostensible subjects, but of the "regulars" who also frequented Gardena card rooms, sometimes at the expense of relationships, jobs, bank accounts, and quality of life. The final chapter of Hayano's book, "And the Days are Just So Many

Decks," is beautifully chilling in its depiction of wasted time as the central facet of the gambling experience for professionals. Hayano makes full-time poker sound anything but glamorous.[2]

The answer as a recreational player certainly isn't to quit playing poker—although that should always be an option if you find yourself stuck in a negative cycle of losing and hating it. But do think about balancing your life whenever poker seems to be dominating too much. Be more like one of Hayano's "occasionals" then a hard-core regular; don't neglect other responsibilities and other pleasures. As I noted in Chapter 3, "Getting Started," playing online can be an especially virulent time-suck. Since it's generally more fun to play in live games than online, it may be a wise choice to cut back on your online play once it's served its purpose as a learning tool, and do more road trips instead.

Personally, I find I enjoy poker more these days after having learned to take it less seriously. I got heavily into it when I was first making the transition from home to casino games, and this was surely the right thing to do. Now that I'm established, however, I prefer to treat poker like any other hobby: there are some months I'll spend a lot of time playing and reading and refining my skills, but other months I put it aside for a while to do other stuff. I always find that when I come back to poker after having been away, I'm fresher and actually play better (that is, as soon as I knock the rust off).

So let's assume you work out, you eat right, and thanks to improved self-knowledge, you tilt about as much as an aircraft carrier on a calm sea; your friends are starting to call you a strong player, but you're looking for ways to get even stronger. Let's turn to the subject of our next and final chapter: refining your game through additional reading, additional thinking, and some new and powerful ideas.

---

2. "Poker Faces" is long out of print, but it's worth chasing down a copy if you can, via any of the used bookstores on the Web.

Chapter 13

Refining Your Game

The great thing about poker as a hobby is there's never any pressure to do more than just have fun. As long as you're comfortable with the stakes you're playing, and are within spitting distance of breaking even over the long haul, you can play for the rest of your life and not worry about theory or technique or what the heck that guy was up to when he reraised you on the flop with just a flimsy drawing hand against your obvious top pair.

But if you *do* want to get better—and you wouldn't have bought this book otherwise—there are plenty of ways to do so. If you like to read, there are lots of great poker books out there to help you; if you don't like to read, you're missing a big resource, but you can still get better by thinking about the game and posting hands on Internet discussion sites.

Not to mention that some of the ideas in this chapter will also point you in the direction of improved play—primarily by demonstrating how you can adapt the basic strategy you've presumably learned by now to suit different game situations. Poker is not a one-size-fits-all game. The better players know this and can fluidly change their style as needed.

Recommended books for hold'em, stud, and other games

Imagine what it was like 20 years ago, when maybe the only truly good book on poker was "Super/System"! Today the poker industry has boomed to the degree that you can get half a dozen great players' advice. It's almost though not quite as good as having a great player as your personal coach. The trick, as always, is to avoid the bad writers and their money-losing advice. You won't go wrong with the books which follow; I've read them all and can highly recommend them. The authors are all widely recognized (not just by me) as solid, reliable, and in many cases, fun to read.[1]

"Hold'em Poker for Advanced Players," by David Sklansky and Mason Malmuth.

This book has much in common with the stud book by the same authors: It's poorly written and organized, and is replete with incomplete or ambigious passages. The authors defend themselves by saying it's the material that's obscure, not their writing, but in truth, they could have used a better editor. Once you get past this kvetch, however, there's no question of their authority or the power of their ideas. Simply put, if you don't read this book, you're in danger of losing to someone who has.

The section on loose games is especially useful for the low-limit player—but only if you realize that Sklansky and Malmuth are talking only about one particular kind of loose game and not all loose games. Their advice here is meant for loose-passive games in which you get many callers both before and after the flop. If you try to apply it to a passive game that's only loose after the flop, with a lot of nervous folding preflop, you'll get killed. (I'll have more to say about that later on in this chapter, under the heading of "Refining your play.") The book's famous hand chart, which attempts to classify starting hands by strength, has been much lampooned—but it contains more dense information than most of us can pack into our heads, and will reward repeated study every few months. For example, I discovered at one point that I was overvaluing KQ in early position; I went back to the hand chart, and it confirmed that KQ *is* a relatively weak hand, much weaker than many low-limit players realize. The chart does a poor job of helping a

---

1. As before, I'm going to avoid the temptation to list bad books. It would probably take too many pages anyway.

new player learn about the concepts that make hold'em hands slide up and down in value depending on situation; the chapters which accompany the chart aren't very clear either, but at least they'll get you thinking in about the right direction.

"Middle Limit Holdem Poker," by Bob Ciaffone and Jim Brier.

This book has drawn a great deal of praise and criticism from various readers posting in online poker forums. In my opinion it's terrific. It's far more readable than anything put out by Sklansky and Malmuth, and it covers all aspects of the game, including a pithy section on short-handed play. Although it's meant for middle-limit games ($10-$20 up to $40-$80), the authors frequently refer to low-limit games by way of comparison, so you can pick up a lot of ideas. You can quibble with some of their advice—for example, in my opinion they harp too much on the danger of small flushes losing to bigger flushes—but they still have much to teach you.

A particularly nice aspect of the book is that the various discussions of different facets of play are followed by a series of problems, like a quiz. This lets you read a problem and think about how you would handle it, before uncovering the answer and seeing how the authors think it should be done. In most cases their depth of thinking will exceed yours.

"The Complete Book of Hold 'Em Poker," by Gary Carson.

This book is more likely to be confusing than helpful for the beginning poker player, so I'd recommend that you avoid it when you're first starting out. Carson writes at a higher level than most beginners can understand, and some of his advice may be flat-out dangerous. For example, he considers King-Jack offsuit (KJo in the vernacular) to be playable in multiway pots against loose players—whereas most experts consider this a death hand in that situation, since a lone pair of Jacks or Kings will usually be drawn out on by loose players ignoring pot odds for a chance to see the turn and even the river. I go with the experts on this one.

All the same, Carson has some interesting ideas—for example, he makes explicit the otherwise implicit models that various authors use in presenting hold'em strategy: "hold'em is a game of money and odds," versus "hold'em is a game of dominated hands," etc.

Finally, if you want to learn to play short-handed, I've found Carson's charts for starting hands in different types of games to be fairly useful, just as long as you've also read the short-handed sections in the Brier/Ciaffone and Sklansky/Malmuth books.

"Positive Expected Value Hold'em Strategy," by Abdul-Jalib M'hall.

Surprise—this isn't a book but a Web site. Abdul-Jalib is reportedly a professional poker player; at any rate, over the years he has posted many ideas, critiques, and diatribes to various poker newsgroups. I know nothing else worth mentioning about the man, but if you want to learn more about hold'em, his Web site is worth taking a look at and even printing out for further reading. I especially recommend his articles on starting hands and drawing odds. The address at the time of writing is www.posev.com/poker/holdem/strategy/index.htm.

"Real Poker: The Cooke Collection" and "Real Poker II: The Play of Hands," both by Roy Cooke with John Bond.

Both these books are collections of Cooke's columns from *Card Player* magazine, and both are worth owning.

The first time I picked up "The Cooke Collection," however, I was disappointed, and in fact didn't think much of the book. Cooke wrote only about hold'em, I saw by thumbing the pages, while I was strictly a stud player. "Why doesn't he write about anything else?" I thought, before putting the book aside.

Two years later I was a confirmed hold'em junkie. Dimly remembering Cooke, I picked him up again—and quickly got lost in the same pages I had previously dismissed as too limited. Cooke (as ghosted through the pen of John Bond) writes engagingly about the thought process of a top player—about, as he puts it, "flowcharting" his options as he plays a hand from beginning to end. If hold'em is your game, Cooke makes for a great role model, even if you'll probably never duplicate his depth of thinking.

Cooke is a great role model (and great reading) for still another reason: he's open about presenting his humiliations in print. Feeling discouraged, he folds on the turn where he should have called—and watches the river card fall that would have won him a monster pot. Trying to impress a pretty girl, he calls when he knows he should fold—and kicks himself for it afterwards, just as we all kick ourselves for dumb plays. Where so many poker writers pretend to be without blemish, Cooke offers himself up as a human being.

Speaking of human frailties, "The Cooke Collection" includes columns addressing the pitfalls of taking poker too seriously and letting it distort your life, while "The Play of Hands" is only about poker at the table. These extra columns are so interesting, and so valuable to the recreational player, that I'd recommend starting with "The Cooke Collection" first.

"Seven Card Stud Poker," by Konstantin Othmer.

If you become a seven-card stud expert, to the degree that "Seven-Card Stud for Advanced Players" is no longer enough to keep your interest, you can consider this book full of complicated looking tables and charts, all concerned with the odds different stud hands face as they duke it out among themselves street-by-street to the river. But while the charts are interesting, and may well be rewarding if you study them hard enough, I don't consider this book a must-read. If you play stud long enough you'll probably get a good feel for most of what Othmer is talking about. Treat it as a potentially useful curiosity and you won't go far wrong.

"The Theory of Poker," by David Sklansky.

Have I not mentioned this book before? Actually, I know I did, in Chapter 1 and again in Chapter 6, but I may not have laid enough stress on it. Get this book and read it. Then put it aside for six months. Then read it again. You still won't really understand it—but keep putting it aside and picking it up. Eventually some of what Sklansky is writing about will sink in.

As I mentioned, the section on common opponent weaknesses and how to exploit them is easily worth the cover price—but so are many other sections. Since the whole book is so important, I'm not going to go into more detail; suffice to say that I'm vexed with Two Plus Two, the publisher, for only putting the book out with a cheap glued binding. The covers fell off my original copy some time ago, so I'm working off my second copy; when the covers fall off that copy as well, as they surely will, I'll have to go and buy a third. A nice-hard cover edition would sell just as well for the publisher and I wouldn't have to keep copying over my hand-penciled margin notes.

There are many other interesting books—far more on hold'em than on stud, unfortunately—but I'll stop here. Once you've really absorbed the books on this list, you'll probably be well enough along in your poker career that you won't need me for a guide anymore.

Thinking, talking, and posting about hands

Aside from book learning, you can learn a lot just by going over hands you've played or misplayed—when I'm at a casino or club, I generally excuse myself from the table long enough to write down two or three such hands for later analysis. A buddy helps here, as long as he's about your level or better, and is equally interested in improving.

The other alternative is to post your hands on Internet discussion groups and get *lots* of comments and advice. Two good groups are the stalwart newsgroup, rec.gambling.poker, and the Two Plus Two forums found at www.twoplustwo.com.

If you frequent these discussion groups, you'll quickly discover that your fellow posters are a mixed lot. Some don't have a clue and yet are convinced they know everything; others are genuine resources with a great deal of hard-won expertise to offer the beginner or intermediate player. When the topic is low-limit poker, though, the typical poster falls somewhere between these two extremes: they're rarely arrogant, and they're rarely that knowledgeable. Most will have read a slew of poker books, yet many will not have understood these books very well.

Be polite when posting your questions and replies—the Internet lends itself to rudeness, whether intentional or not. I've been guilty of the latter on occasion, especially when dealing with posters who I've assumed were more knowledgeable then they later prove to be. If this happens, I do my best to apologize fully, even if I feel some of the blame lies on their side. It's not worth creating hard feelings in this setting.

If you're posting a question about a hand, be sure to include all relevant information, including the size of the pot, the character of the game, what you knew or didn't know about your chief opponents, and the limit. If you can, check your post for typos before sending it—a little detail like typing KQs instead of KJs can make a big difference. You'll see many examples of good posts to copy once you start browsing the groups regularly.

If I have a complaint about these groups, it's that too many posters seem overly concerned with their results from individual hands—even when the hands are routine. Posters of this sort seem to be asking for reassurance more than anything else.

The posts I value, on the other hand, are where someone has put in some thought and is asking a genuinely interesting question, often about some quirky aspect of strategy or tactics. You'll occasionally find posters who are so knowledgeable and experienced that they can persuasively argue that a given book or author is wrong on a particular topic. That's when these discussion groups really get fun. And of course, many expert authors are themselves contributors to the discussions, albeit usually on advanced topics. You'll find David Sklansky, Ray Zee, Lee Jones, Mike Caro, and others posting interesting stuff if you have the time to troll. Many posts have been archived, too, and Web searches can turn up some great hits. For example, I first heard of Morton's Theorem as the result of a search of archived posts. For all I know no one has written yet about this theorem in a poker book, and yet it's a fascinating idea.[2]

Examples of refining your play

We've come to the heart of this chapter. I want to give you an idea of the kinds of adjustments you'll find yourself making, and in fact *having* to make, once you get eyes to see. When you're first starting out in public poker, everything is such a novelty that you can only cope with things one at a time. You assume that beating a low-limit stud game one time means you can beat it again if you get decent cards—and yet when you come back, you get those good cards but you lose. What's going on?

Usually, the game conditions have changed. Maybe the table is tighter, maybe it's looser. Maybe a smart, aggressive player is

---

2. Stripped of its fancy math, Morton's Theorem says that a good hand competing against many bad hands should root for at least some of the bad hands to fold rather than call, even if said calls are theoretically incorrect. It's like a super version of *reverse implied odds*. The theorem was the work of Andy Morton, an L.A.-based poker player who died young in a motorcycle crash.

getting you off balance, or a passive, weak player is calling you down and beating some bluffs you got away with against tighter players. Because you're a situational player, you need to change also. Everything I'm going to show you here is an example of a change and how you might respond. The examples range from the trivial to the not-so-trivial, but that's not important—what *is* important is this notion of constant adjustment, constant questioning, constant refining. Yesterday's strategy and tactics were fine for yesterday's game; what you need to know is how you should play right now.

Adjusting to a different limit

Let's say you've gotten comfortable with the tiny $1-$3 stud game played at some of the casinos on the East Coast. (You don't want to linger too long at this limit, since the rake is evil and the lack of an ante teaches you to play the opposite of how you'll play at the bigger limits—but that's another topic.) Now you're flying out to Las Vegas, where you hear they spread the same no-ante game, only with a limit of $1-$5. Do you need to adjust to this extra $2? Does it make a real difference?

The answers are yes and yes. That extra two dollars makes it much easier to manipulate the bet size to your liking. You can drop players by bringing down a $5 hammer on Fourth Street if you've got a hand that prefers only one or two opponents, or you can limp in cheaply on Third Street with something like a small pocket pair, knowing that if you get lucky on Fourth Street you'll be able to build a good pot to compensate for all the times you don't hit trips. As we noted in our discussion of playing tight in Chapter 4, you probably wouldn't even play a small pocket pair at your usual limit of $1-$3, solely because of the smaller bet size.

Spend a little time thinking about this sort of thing ahead of time, and you'll catch on that much faster once your plane has touched down and you're seated at the table; forget to think about it at all, and you'll miss such opportunities no matter how much table time you put in.

Getting a feel for bluffing

When you're first following the rigid guidelines you've inherited from Lee Jones or Roy West, you won't be doing much bluffing. Both Jones and West stress that bluffs aren't the way to win at the low limits, and they're right. But if you *never* bluff, you'll not only start passing up pots you could have won, but become easy prey once you edge up in limit and have to face better players. Here are some tips to get you started:

Some games cry out for bluffing, especially against weak opponents. My favorite for this is a game never played in casinos, but commonly played in home games: Seven-stud high-low declare. Because of the declare, you can murder this game by raising early with a scary low board, even if you've got big cards in the hole. This gives you two ways to win: First, if no one else picks up a decent low, you'll go unchallenged and will pick up the low half of the pot without even having to show your hand. Second, your early raises frequently will drive out players with middling cards who could easily have picked up a low to beat you. The key here is being able to read the other players and fold quickly when you sense someone has a real low going.

Note that weak, passive players won't have a clue about all the pots you're stealing, because a) they only bluff on late streets themselves, never early streets; b) they don't understand the use of raises to knock out other players early, and c) they play their own cards, not the situation, hence certain moves become impossible for them. And if a move is impossible for them, they can't imagine you making it either.

Head-up situations call for bluffing more often. See Chapter 8 for a discussion of short-handed bluffing in hold'em; stud has fewer such opportunities, because each player has his own board, but you still need to bet or raise more often with scare cards than you would in a multi-way pot. This is especially true if the deal started short-handed: with fewer players dealt in, it's less likely that anyone has a strong hand. Moreover, if a weak player doesn't hold decent cards, he's more likely to concede the loss of what he can see for himself is a small pot. All of this calls for more aggression on your part, and more aggression with poor cards means more bluffs and semi-bluffs.

You can often bluff an opponent off a weak hand, but rarely off a hand he likes. Many novice players pick the worst times to bluff: They'll raise or reraise representing a monster, not noticing that one opponent or another has fallen in love with his hand and intends to call with it no matter what. The time to bluff weak players is when they're clearly dubious about their hands and are eager to believe you have something better. From their point of view, your bet or raise is saving them the trouble of losing more money with bad cards.

Against good opponents, you bluff often enough that they're forced to call your good hands too. As mentioned, a good player isn't like a calling station; if you only bet or raise with your good hands, he'll soon realize this and never call you except when he has a good shot at beating you. Therefore you need to occasionally bet or raise with more speculative hands; this might be an occasional pure bluff, but is more likely to be a semi-bluff with a long-shot draw or a small pair with additional outs. Occasionally a raise or reraise on a cheap street is effectively a bluff; you're setting it up so that a scare card or even making your long-shot hand gives you extra options against this good opponent. Sometimes you're representing a monster and you actually make the monster; other times you'll take a free card or else quietly fold.

Not raising early in loose games, so as to keep the pot small

With certain types of very loose players—for example, players who chase to the river in hold'em with something as weak as bottom pair or a single overcard—you're often better not raising on early streets with hands that would normally justify it.

An example would be not raising with AQ in early position in a very loose-passive hold'em game. A raise wouldn't knock out enough players that you could possibly hope to win with an Ace-high if the flop didn't come with an Ace or Queen. More to the point, even if the flop *does* pair you, you still don't love it if several of these loose players insist on clinging to you like fruit flies till the river. There is just too great a chance one of these gnats is going to make a cheap two pair and deprive you of the pot.

In this situation, not raising before the flop helps in two ways: First, with the pot kept small, players who chase with a hand like bottom pair will be making a bigger mistake than usual, since they'll be further than ever from positive expectation. But more importantly for you, by not giving your hand away you preserve the ability to knock players out on the flop by raising or check-raising, or possibly waiting to raise on the turn. Even the loosest of loose players will reluctantly fold bottom pair or a gutshot draw if faced with a double bet. Had you raised pre-flop, on the other hand, it might get checked around to you on the flop, depriving you of this leverage.

I'm here to tell you that these sorts of plays not only work, but are a *necessity* for certain low-limit games where one-pair hands must be handled gingerly and often folded, even if they're clearly the best hand in the early going.

Raising early in loose games, so as to thin the field

Surprise! As I mentioned earlier in this chapter in my review of the Sklansky/Malmuth hold'em book, there's more than one type of loose game—and if you don't adjust for the differences, you'll be giving your money away.

I haven't seen it written about a lot, but there are certain hold'em games on the Internet—at the $2/$4 and $3/$6 limits in particular—that play tight and passive before the flop, but loose and passive after the flop. I'm not certain why this is, but in such games, standard loose-game strategies fall apart, including the one advocated by Sklansky and Malmuth in "Hold'em Poker for Advanced Players."

In a very loose-passive game, you typically try to play a lot more drawing hands and don't raise as much with hands like AQ and AK, since the latter end up getting hurt by their reverse implied odds with all those loose players calling. However, in a tight-passive game, there are rarely enough players seeing the flop to justify limping in with speculative drawing hands such as King-little suited, Ace-little suited, medium suited connectors, and so on. This is true even though after the flop the game turns quite loose, with players calling to the river with gutshot draws, Ace high, bottom pair, and so on. A pre-flop raise from under the gun often wins the blinds, but no more; even a late raise may only get one or two callers. So where's your profit in this situation?

It turns out that rather than limping with a lot of drawing hands and throwing away your offsuit cards, you should do the reverse: rarely play drawing hands, and do a lot of open-raising, even with weak big-card hands like KQ and KJ. Even your suited big cards are often better raised than limped, though in this case you can now start raising behind limpers rather than just open-raising. What you're hoping to do is drive out nervous hands that are better than yours, such as AJ and even a downstream AQ, while either stealing the blinds or getting just one or two callers on the flop. If you're a good player, these short-handed flops give you a big advantage against easily readable opponents—if someone gives signs of having a real hand, you fold; if you missed against a passive calling station, he'll check behind you to the river; if you connect and he doesn't, he'll pay you off the whole way, giving you your profit; and so on. If you get reraised before the flop, or get a call from someone you know is a very tight player, you can guess that your relatively weak raising hand is probably beat, and you'll fold if you don't hit a great flop. Additionally, you'll probably want to limp early with AA, KK, and other pairs as well, so as to have a shot at winning more then the blinds with these powerhouses.

In summary, I hope these few examples have given you some ideas for how a grasp of poker concepts can let you adapt your basic strategy to new conditions. As I've said before, the better you can adapt, the more you'll win in the long run from opponents who can't. You'll also have more fun and be able to play in a wider range of games.

Going back to your home game with your new skills

We've come to the end of the book, though not to the end of your development as a player. I hope you never completely shed your home-game roots: public poker is fun, but it's more costly, usually involves more time and travel, and can never be as relaxed and companionable as playing cards with guys (and gals) you know and like.

So what's a recreational poker player to do when he finds his skills have outgrown that comfy old home game? Personally, I rarely play anymore with friends who aren't pretty hard-core about poker; I do it now and then as a social thing, but it's hard to restrain my instinct to go for the jugular and I don't want to have to try.

Nor do I live near enough my old home game in Hastings, New York to play in it regularly anymore. I still visit now and then, and if I could play regularly I think I would; it's a good group and there's a lot of laughter. I could never go as hog-wild about it I once did, however, back when I used to ponder starting hands and strategy for games like Baseball, Chicago with Power, Iron Cross, and the like.

If, unlike me, you're able to keep playing in your original home game, you'll likely find that you can now read your regular opponents and their betting patterns very clearly. They won't be reading you any better than before, so this factor alone will give you a big edge. And if your group perchance plays a few odd-ball games, it can't hurt to spend just a *little* time thinking about good strategy. This will give still more edge, since few if any of the other players will take poker this seriously.

All this edge you've accumulated has to be dealt with delicately, of course; your goal in this setting is more social than anything else. I don't have to tell you to loosen up more than you would if you wanted just to win, since this is obvious.

If in spite of all this you find yourself yawning at key junctures in your home game, here are two ideas to liven things up:

•   If you've been playing nickel-ante stakes, make some quiet inquiries to see if you can get together a limit more like $1/$2. It's not much more money, and it'll keep you more amused than calling all those five-cent raises. (We call five-cent raises "snivels" in the Hastings game, since they're usually thrown in by someone who should have already folded, but wants to reach the three-raise maximum cheaply so he can see just one more card.) The only danger here is that you don't want to break up the original game by drawing off too many players; if that seemed likely, I would drop my bid for a higher limit to preserve the peace.

- Here's a related idea I've been toying with, but haven't yet put into practice: Find some buddies who are willing to experiment with pot-limit poker. Now, *that* would be interesting. I've never played pot-limit, but they spread a pot-limit game at one of the clubs; maybe when I grow up I'll have a big enough bankroll to sit in, and by that time maybe I'll have played enough hands in a pot-limit home game that I'll be ready. Even a nickel for an ante would be enough to give rise to some real pot-limit action, where a bluff is no laughing matter but something to be gravely weighed, and you can rob someone of all his chips, or be robbed yourself, in the space of a single hand.

Either of these ideas is enough to keep me dreaming; until then, see you at the card table!

Glossary

Advertise. To bluff or play loosely and let others know it, in hopes of getting calls later on with legitimate hands.

Aggressive. Prone to betting and raising. Can be a good or bad quality depending on whether the player is *tough* or just a *maniac*.

All-in. To call a bet with all the money you have on the table; under most house rules, you cannot put more money on the table until the hand is over. Going all-in is commonplace for no-limit games, but good limit players avoid it because it deprives them of further leverage.

Ante. In games like stud and draw, the small amount put into the pot by each player prior to cards being dealt. It is equivalent to a blind bet, but most players don't stop to think of it in those terms.

Baby. A small card, generally a Deuce, Three, or Four: "I had a baby pocket pair."

Bad beat. A hand during which you are playing well and deservedly crushing your opponent, but the fool stays in against overwhelming odds to *draw out* on you with a *miracle card*.

Bankroll. Money you only play poker with. Most recreational players don't keep a strict bankroll, but it's a good idea to start.

Bet into. To take the initiative and bet first against an opponent who showed strength on an earlier *street*. When passive players bet into you for no apparent reason, you know they've got a big hand.

Bicycle. See *wheel*.

Big blind. The player two seats to the left of the dealer in hold'em who must make a forced bet equal to the opening bet prior to cards being dealt.

Blank. A card that doesn't help a player's hand; in common card games like hold'em or Omaha, a card that seems unlikely to have helped anyone at all.

Blinds. The forced bets made by the two players to the immediate left of the dealer (the *button*) in hold'em, prior to hole cards being dealt. Typically there is a big blind and a little blind, the former equal to one small bet and the latter equal to some fraction thereof, such as one-third or one-half.

Board. Cards dealt up as part of the game. In common-card games such as hold'em and Omaha, cards on the board can be used by any player; in games such as seven-card stud, each player has their own board. In the latter case, poker writers sometimes use *board* to refer to all the players' boards considered as a whole.

Bring-in. In seven-card stud, a small forced bet paid by the low card showing after the first three cards are dealt.

Button. The plastic disk used in hold'em and Omaha to denote the player who is now *dealer* and therefore acts last in each betting round after the flop. "The button raised with pocket Kings."

Buy-in. The minimum amount of chips you must purchase to sit down at a house game in a casino or club.

Check-raise. To check the first time around, then raise if it is bet behind you. A powerful weapon with diverse purposes when used properly.

Chop. In hold'em, if the table folds around to the blinds, the little blind and big blind can agree to chop, meaning they simply take back their blinds rather than play out the hand head-up. Chopping makes a certain amount of horse sense, especially at the low limits where the rake is big in proportion to the bet size. If your neighbor proposes to chop with you, you may want to agree if it keeps him happy—happy players are more likely to gamble it up. There is no obligation to chop, however, especially if you want more practice playing head-up or stealing.

Cold. As in, "I couldn't believe it—he called three bets *cold* with Seven-Five *offsuit!*" To call a raise or reraise without having first called the initial bet. A sign either of a strong hand or a bad player.

Come hand. A drawing hand such as a flush or straight; to be *on the come* is to be drawing to such a hand.

Counterfeit. A term usually applied to community card games like Omaha, in which you can have the best hand until a card is dealt that you already hold—it is of no use to you, but makes possible a lower low or a higher high for someone else. You have been counterfeited.

Cutoff. In hold'em, the player immediately before the *dealer*. A significant position because if the cutoff can raise and get the dealer to fold, the cutoff will now enjoy the privilege of being last to act on each *street* after the *flop*.

Dealer. Normally, the person dealing the cards—but in hold'em or Omaha, the player who has the *button* for each hand and is therefore last to act.

Dog. Short for underdog; refers to your poor chances of winning. Sometimes used with a specific set of odds, as in, "I figured I was an 8 to 1 dog." See *favorite*.

Draw out on. To beat an opponent by catching a card on a late *street*.

Drawing dead. Attempting to complete a hand such as a straight when it will likely loose to a bigger hand, for example a flush.

Expectation. A mathematical term commonly used in poker to signify whether in the long run, a given play will make or cost you money. Commonly we speak of a winning play as having *positive expectation* and a losing play as having *negative expectation*.

Fastplay. To aggressively bet or raise a hand on an early *street* rather than later on. Most players with very strong hands prefer to slowplay them, but fastplaying, by going against expectations, can sometimes earn more money.

Favorite. A hand favored by the odds to win. See *dog*.

Fill. Short for fill up, meaning to catch a card that turns two pair or trips into a full house.

Fish. A player so inferior to the other players in the game that he represents a guaranteed source of income. Note the inferiority is relative, not absolute.

Flat-call. Also smooth-call. To call a bet or raise without raising or reraising, especially when holding a powerful hand.

Flop. The first three community cards in hold'em; followed by the *turn* and *river*. To flop a hand is to complete it using these three cards plus your hole cards, needing no help from either turn or river: "He flopped the *nut* straight."

Gutshot, gut. An inside straight.

Head-up, heads-up. Doyle Brunson prefers head-up, but David Sklansky prefers heads-up; either way, a hand or game involving only two players.

Implied odds. A variation of *pot odds*. With more cards to come, you are hoping to buy a card cheaply now that could make you a *monster* later and gain you many future bets. In other words, with implied odds, you take into consideration not just the money currently in the pot, but the money that may be in the pot at the end of the hand. See also *reverse implied odds.*

Jam. To raise and reraise until the maximum number of bets has been reached for a particular *street.*

Kill. A game with a kill is one in which the bet limit doubles under certain conditions—for example, if the preceding pot exceeded a specified size, or if the same player has won two hands in a row. In games like Omaha and hold'em, the winner in a kill game usually posts a *kill blind,* equal to twice the amount of the big blind; all who wish to play must at least see the kill blind, with the usual option to raise. Note that some games are played with a half-kill or even a quarter-kill.

Loose. A player who plays too many starting hands, calls too many raises, or goes too far with the hands he plays. See *tight.*

Maniac. A player who bets and raises so freely as to either go bankrupt quickly, if he's catching bad cards, or bankrupt everyone else, if he's catching good cards.

Miracle card. An unlikely card that would give you the winner and for which you are praying; for example, the one card in the deck that can complete an inside straight-flush draw.

Monster. A hand of immense strength. Can vary according to the situation; a monster *head-up* against the *big blind* might be no better than cat food if played *under the gun.*

Negative expectation. A play (whether a call, fold, check, bet, or raise) that in the long run loses you money. See *expectation.*

Nut, nuts. The best hand currently possible: "The King gave him the nut full house, but then the Ace on the *river* gave the other guy the nuts instead."

Offsuit. As opposed to suited. Used when speaking of hole cards in hold'em.

On the come. See *come hand.*

Out. When more cards are to come, a card that improves your hand. A *clean out* helps just you; a *tainted out* helps you, but also gives an opponent a better hand.

Passive. A player who won't *play back* at you unless he has a *monster.* See *aggressive.*

Pick up. See *steal.*

Play back. To respond to a bet with a raise or reraise. Generally used in situations where the first player may be trying to *steal* or *pick up* the antes or blinds.

Pocket. Cards held in the pocket, or down; for example, a pocket pair in hold'em, or your two down cards in stud.

Position. The order in which players are to act on a particular *street.* In hold'em games, position is determined in relation to the dealer *button* that travels around the table; in stud games it's determined by who has the highest hand showing. Position can be early or late.

Positive expectation. A play (whether a call, fold, check, bet, or raise) that in the long run makes you money. See *expectation.*

Pot odds. The ratio of the money currently in the pot to the size of the bet facing you; generally contrasted with the odds of improving to the winning hand with the next card dealt.

Price. The cost of buying a card now, in relation to how much money you might win if you make the hand you're aiming for. An old-school term that deserves more usage, since it speaks so clearly to the notion of *implied odds.*

Quads. Four-of-a-kind.

Rag, rags. See *blank*.

Reverse implied odds. A variation of *pot odds* in which a good situation can only get worse. Specifically, you have started with a strong hand but one that can't improve easily, such as a pair of Aces; if many players stay in to draw against you with hands such as straights and flushes, they collectively make you a *dog*—hence you have reverse implied odds.

River. The fifth and last common card dealt in hold'em or in Omaha; also used, though less often, to apply to the seventh card dealt to each player in seven-stud. To *river* an opponent or a hand is to make the winning hand with the last card.

Rolled up. To be dealt three-of-a-kind, or *trips*, as your first three cards in seven-card stud.

Semi-bluff. To bet or raise with a hand that is not the best now, but has potential to improve to the best hand.

Set. In hold'em, *trips* in which two of the three cards are your hole cards; thus, you must be holding a *pocket* pair to make a set. They're better than trips because they're concealed.

Slowplay. To call on an early *street* with a very strong hand, rather than raise and frighten opponents out. However, it's not a slowplay if you don't put in the raise at some point; merely calling on the river with your powerful hand makes you *passive*.

Small blind. Also called the little blind. The player immediately to the left of the *dealer* in hold'em, who must make a small forced bet prior to cards being dealt; this bet is usually one-third or one-half the size of the opening bet.

Steal. To attempt to win the *antes* or *blinds* without a struggle, by raising with a high card showing or in late position.

Steaming. On *tilt*.

Street. The stages of a poker hand as represented by how many cards have been dealt. For example, Third Street in seven-card stud represents the first three cards, two down and one up, dealt to all players; Seventh Street is the seventh and final card dealt.

Stuck. Losing at the moment.

Switch gears. To change from one style to another during the course of a game—for example, to go from *loose* to *tight*, or from *slowplaying* to *fastplaying*.

Tight. A player who folds a lot of starting hands, calls few raises, or folds fairly often on early streets. Can be good or bad; see *weak-tight*.

Tilt. A term borrowed with its meaning largely intact from pinball. Most recreational players tend to go on tilt after too many *bad beats*, or if they've gotten *stuck*. Every hand looks playable, every raise callable, and the chips flow like a river into the sea.

Tough. Hard to read, hard to intimidate; capable of tight yet *aggressive* play. See *weak*.

Trash. Terrible starting cards which poker authorities advise you not to play, but which your opponents often seem to show down on the *river* for a winning two pair, etc.

Tricky. A player who regularly uses deceptive plays such as slow-playing, semi-bluffing, bluffing, or varying tactics. Tricky players usually make for more difficult opponents, even if they're too tricky for their own good. See *tough*, *weak*.

Trips. Three-of-a-kind.

Turn. The turn card is the fourth common card dealt in hold'em. To turn a hand is to make it when this card appears: "He turned a flush."

Under the gun. The player first to act in highly positional games such as hold'em, Omaha, and five-card draw.

Variance. The inevitable ups and downs in *bankroll* due to the randomness of cards. Variance from a hypothetical norm can be calculated mathematically if good records are kept for a reasonable amount of time, typically 100 hours or more.

Weak. Easily read and easily intimidated. See *tough*.

Weak-tight. A player who is trying to play well by not calling too much, but who has now gone too far in the other direction and folds too easily on later streets. Such players are easily manipulated by aggressive opponents.

Wheel. A straight from Ace to Five. In games where straights don't count against a low hand, a wheel is the ultimate low; such a low hand is also called a bicycle or bike.

Wired. Same as *pocket* pair. Usually used only in seven-card stud, where you get two down cards and an up card, even though you also get two down cards in hold'em.

Index

A
addiction 134
angle-shooter 16
ante 52
B
bad advice 58
bad beats 131
bad luck 130
bankroll requirements 34
beginner books 58
Bellagio 15
betting structure 52, 55
big-hand statues 112
bluffing 145
board 99
Bond, John 139
breaks 21
Bridgeport Post 164
Brier, Jim 61
Brunson, Doyle 5, 63
buy-in 20
buying in 29
C
calling station 79, 82
Card Player magazine 139
cardroom seduction 129
Caro, Mike 5, 71, 109, 143
Carson, Gary 138
chip-grabbers 111
Ciaffone, Bob 34, 61, 64
collusion 19, 31
ConJelCo 27, 165
Cooke, Roy 139

D
Damon, Matt 83
de Méré, Chevalier 37
dominated hand 57
drawing dead 44
draws 51
drunks 84
E
Education of a Poker Player 4
effective odds 36, 49
etiquette 15
expectation 37
F
fatigue 127
fixed-limit 55
Foxwoods Casino 4
G
Gambling Theory and Other
Topics 58
game selection 124
going all-in 20
H
habits and weaknesses 76
hand protection 17
Hartford Courant 164
Hayano, David 134
hold'em 23, 59, 61, 85
home games 51, 77, 149
home poker vs. casino poker
13
hourly rate 33
House of Games 109

I

implied odds 36, 40, 41, 55
Internet Poker 27
Internet poker 36

J

Jalib, Abdul 44, 139
Jones, Lee 58, 61, 143

K

Kasparov, Garry 126
Krieger, Lou 27

L

Lee 143
long run 37
long-term expectation 40
loose vs. tight 80

M

Malmuth, Mason 9, 34, 58,
60, 99, 109
maniac 82
micro-limits 32
Mirage 15
misdeclares 18
Mohegan Sun 85
Morton's Theorem 143
muck 17

N

naïve vs. knowledgeable 80
negative variance 33
NetTeller 30
newsgroup 29
no-limit 24, 55

O

obsession 134
odds 36, 40, 41, 45
Omaha high-low 23
online poker 24, 27, 28, 30,
31
Othmer, Konstantin 140
outs 36, 40, 45

P

Packel, Edward 37
Paradise Poker 28, 29, 30, 73
Pascal, Blaise 37
passive vs. aggressive 80
play money 29
player tendencies 100
playing not tight enough 120
playing tight 56
playing too loose 119
playing too passive 119
poker as a hobby 136
Poker Faces 134
PokerStars 29
PokerStat 30
positive expectation 9, 37
pot odds 40, 41, 45
pot-limit 24, 55
premature folders 112
probability theory 37

R

rake 23, 52, 54
reading hands 68
rec.gambling.poker 29, 142
record keeping 32
recreational poker 149
refining your play 143
regular or local 83
reverse implied odds 36, 40,
42
rituals 14
rock 79, 81
Rounders 83
rules 14

S
scare-card bettors 103
self-weighting 9
Seven Card Stud 6
seven card stud 23, 59, 99
Seven-card Stud for Advanced Players 5
short-handed 94
showdown 18
side-pot 20
situationally based play 8
Sklansky, David 6, 34, 44, 60, 62, 118, 143
slow-play 94
slumming mid-limit player 84
software 25
splash the pot 17
spread-limit 23, 55
StatKing 32
steal the blinds 94
Steiner, Peter O. 5
strategy mistakes 119
string bets 16
structured limit 23
Super/System 5

T
tainted outs 43
taking notes 30
telegraphs 111
tells 67, 109, 110
    avoiding 114

The Mathematics of Games and Gambling 37
theory 35
Theory of Poker 6
Thursday Night Poker 5
tilt 82, 130
tipping 19
tourist 83
Turbo 7-Card Stud 25
Turbo Hold'em 11
Turbo Omaha High-Low Split 25
Turbo Stud 11
Turbo Texas Hold'em 25
Two Plus Two forums 142

V
variance 33

W
Watterson, Kathleen Keller 27
West, Roy 6, 43, 44, 59, 99
Wilson Software 25
www.posev.com 139
www.twoplustwo.com 28, 29, 142

Y
Yardley, Herbert 4
young aggressive 83

Z
Zee, Ray 60, 63, 143

About the Author

R andy Burgess has been a professional writer all his adult life, first as a reporter for the *Bridgeport Post* and *Hartford Courant* newspapers, and currently as a freelance marketing writer for the information technology industry. He first played nickel-ante poker with friends from the newsroom in his twenties and thirties; only when he was past forty did the poker bug seriously bite. He has read more poker books than anyone else he knows, including many no longer in print. Since becoming a successful $3/$6 hold'em player, he has recently moved up in limit to $4/$8 and $5/$10. He also enjoys success at low-limit 7-card stud. Currently he lives in Woodstock, New York.

About the Publisher

ConJelCo specializes in books and software for the serious gambler. In addition to this book, ConJelCo publishes *Winning Low-Limit Hold'em* by Lee Jones, *Hold'em Excellence: From Beginner to Winner* by Lou Krieger, *More Hold'em Excellence: A Winner for Life* by Lou Krieger, *Internet Poker: How to Play and Beat Online Poker Games*, by Lou Krieger and Kathleen Keller Watterson, *Winning Omaha/8 Poker* by Mark Tenner and Lou Krieger, *Serious Poker* by Dan Kimberg, as well as *Las Vegas Blackjack Diary* by Stuart Perry, and *Video Poker—Optimum Play* by Dan Paymar. ConJelCo also publishes software including *Blackjack Trainer* for the Macintosh and Windows, *Ken Elliott's CrapSim* for DOS, and *StatKing* for Windows (gambling record keeping software).

We periodically publish a newsletter, *The Intelligent Gambler*, sent free to our customers. *The Intelligent Gambler* carries articles by our authors as well as other respected authors in the gambling community. In addition, it is the source of information about new ConJelCo products and special offers.

We also sell books, software and videos from other publishers. If you'd like a free catalog or to be put on the mailing list for *The Intelligent Gambler* you can write to us at:

> ConJelCo
> 1460 Bennington Ave.
> Pittsburgh, PA 15217

Our phone number is 800-492-9210 (412-621-6040 outside of the U.S.), and our fax number is 412-621-6214.

ConJelCo, and its catalog, is on the Internet. Visit us at *http://www.conjelco.com* or e-mail us at at *orders@conjelco.com*.